Jack Blane

A Life Well Lived

Jean Flannery
and
Jack Blane

Copyright © 2021 Jean Flannery
All rights reserved.
ISBN: 9798738921995

DEDICATION

Dedicated to the memory of my father. Also dedicated to everyone who played a part in his life, especially those who loved him, and to his descendants.

Jean Blane Flannery

CONTENTS

Acknowledgements	5
Foreword	7

JACK

Interview		
Early Years		9
Wartime		24
Post-war	Bletchley	31
	Stewartby	33
Jack Blane's War		41
Jack Adds to Wartime Memories		47
Images		53
Grandfather Altered Our Name		62
Notes on the Blane Family History		64

JEAN

Life in Post-war Britain	68
Back to Jack's Life	94
Later Years	103
A Treasured Family Legacy	111
In Memoriam	112

A MISCELLANY

Picture Gallery	114
Family Myths	154
Family Facts	157
Family Records	165
Family Line	208

What's in a Name?	215
Maps	225
Aylesbury	236
Bletchley	243
Stewartby Village	252
Pre-decimal Currency	260
Imperial Measures	264
Afterword	267
Resources	269

ACKNOWLEDGMENTS

With grateful thanks to all who appear in this book, to those who inspired me to write it, and to Bedford Borough Council's Marston Vale Oral History Project for the interview with my father.

Thanks also to others who aided and abetted me in completing this book.

My sister Carole, who shares family memories, searched out old photos and documents. Her daughter Dawn scanned and sent them to me with results from her own research and those of Rob Schafer, historian extraordinaire.

Honor (Whiting) Lewington, a friend from Stewartby Days, not only proofread for me but kindly looked out and forwarded more information and photos.

Judi Heavens added another pair of eyes, also being kind enough to proofread.

I am grateful to these, to my immediate family, niece Claire, and to all who made suggestions and who encouraged me in this endeavour.

Finally, my grateful thanks as ever to John for his unfailing love, support and patience.

Jean Blane Flannery

FOREWORD

My father, Jack Blane, was born in the closing months of WWI. He saw action from beginning to end of WWII. Afterwards he only wanted a peaceful life, his family at the heart of it.

The first part of this book is told in my father's own words, both spoken and written. It begins with a transcript of his interview recorded 4 July 2001 for the Marston Vale Oral History Project, which was sponsored by Bedford Borough Council.

I have written the interview as a narrative: lightly edited, changing the order slightly, and omitting the interviewer's questions. Some she repeated, some were closed questions. At times she interrupted my father. Due to these interjections I'm afraid that the narrative is still rather disjointed in places.

I have added Dad's own very basic written record of his WWII service, written for his grandchildren, and some other memories and writings of his.

My own writings continue his story and that of his family. Yet I know that there is so much more still to be told.

Some later chapters contain much from my two previous books. So if you have read either of those and recognise the content, please forgive me and read on.

Photographs, documents and maps all help to chart my father's life and times, and his family history.

Comments in italics are always mine.

Errors are also mine, and mine alone, especially given that I've altered and added to this book since the kind efforts of my proof readers.

Jean Blane Flannery

JACK

INTERVIEW

EARLY YEARS

Bletchley Road 1920

I was born at Bletchley on the 14th of August 1918. We were a large family: eight siblings, Mum and Dad, in a three-bedroom house. We sometimes slept three to a bed. As we all grew up we were looked after well by Mum and Dad.

I left school at fourteen and worked for the Cooperative Society of Bletchley for six months, taking milk round to the ladies. You didn't collect any money. You were paid with a check. There were bread checks and milk checks (*pre-purchased plastic tokens*).

After six months I gained worked as an office boy for the London Brick Company and Forders Ltd at their Bletchley works.

My father was born the 11th of July 1880, at Haslingfield in Cambridgeshire. His name was Charles. He worked as an engine driver on the railway.

I cannot remember any of my grandparents. In fact, one on my mother's side I would never have known. But on my father's side, I probably saw them once at their home in Barton, near Cambridge.

My mother's mother eventually died in the Aylesbury Women's Convict Prison. But she wasn't a convict, she was the Matron - and I have evidence, newspaper cuttings, to prove that.

She died long before I was born and before my parents married. My mother met Dad at Aylesbury and they got married at Aylesbury Parish Church (*St Mary's*).

My mother was born the 15th of July in 1878 at Rotherhithe, near the docks. Her name was May Elizabeth Mary Fraser Powell.

She went to school in Paradise Street in London and must have been bright because at fourteen years old Mother started teaching (*as a pupil teacher*).

I don't know very much else about her childhood. She was an only child of her parents. I didn't ask her very much about her life and now I wish I had done, because when I started all of this (*family history*) I can go back to my great grandfather...

It was a very, very poor area, Rotherhithe, a London docks area, and she would have anything up to forty or probably fifty children to teach, little children.

In that area some of them were so poor that the girls didn't have knickers on, and things like that. Paradise Street was a lovely name but I think it was a misnomer!

On Saturdays my mother had to go for her own lessons at school. She became a qualified schoolteacher after serving four years' apprenticeship in the Christ Church National Infants School, ending in January 1897.

Then she moved to Great Hampden in Buckinghamshire. She was an assistant mistress in the Hampden National School, Great and Little Hampden, Bucks, from the 13th September 1897 to the 13th September 1898. But we have no further record until she married in 1904. (*I found a record in the 1901 census. See Family Facts and Records.*)

Great Hampden schoolteachers, with May Powell second from right.

The Hampden school was very countrified. The Lord of the Manor - this is one thing that some people might remember - when the Lord and Lady of the Manor visited the school, the children all had to jump up and say, "Good morning my Lord. Good morning my Lady."

Mother said the only time they had holidays was at harvest time, so that the children could go and help with the harvest.

I presume that otherwise they went to school all year round. One doesn't really know about that sort of thing. If you look back in history about this sort of life, when the children were quite young the parents would take them out of school to work if they couldn't afford to live.

Mother had to give up teaching, as you did in those days, when she and father married on the 15th February 1904. At that time, they both lived at 46 Park Street, Aylesbury.

The witnesses to the marriage were Dad's parents, Charles and Jane Blane. According to the marriage certificate mother's father, Henry Normal Powell was deceased (*that's another story, see Family Myths and Family Facts*) as was her mother.

However, her grandmother Margaret Miller was still alive. She lived in Aylesbury with mother and father, and moved with them to Bletchley, where they first lived on Railway Terrace.

I don't remember any of that. I was the next to youngest of the eight, my sister Margaret being about the middle. And I was born after the family moved to Brooklands Road.

Railway Terrace 1913
May holds Bob. Front: Henry, Don, Charles.
May's grandmother Miller (died 1916) behind

Life was quite easy for us. My father was in work and as we boys grew up we all got jobs and contributed.

My mother always said there is no such word as "can't," and I've heard that recently.

When I left school my writing was atrocious. So mother made me go to W H Smith and Sons (*a stationery chain*) and get a book printed by Burroughs. On each page there were about three blocks of six lines. The first was a line from Aesop's Fables.

There was a list, a picture, of various types of writing. When I had chosen the one I wanted to do my mother, although I'd left school, made me copy all those through. By that means I became quite a good writer.

But my mother wasn't strict. She was a nice Mum.

Mother was always a good cook. Times were sometimes hard but we'd always got plenty of vegetables.

My father had an allotment where he grew all our vegetables. He also kept chickens and probably a rabbit or two in a hutch. We always lived well, never went hungry.

Jack's Dad in the large back garden, with his hen run and coop (far back). He grew flowers as well as fruit and vegetables, loved his chrysanthemums.

Our home was in a row of terraced houses, the terraces going down the road. There were in those days lots of fields to play in. It was easy to play in the road or wherever.

Nobody bothered much as long as you didn't damage things. The children today can't do that. It's an entirely different world.

We had a lot of freedom as children. We could wander down and go along the brook (*which gave the road its name*) or go bird nesting or…

(*Interrupted by interviewer who asked what bird nesting was*).

We looked for birds' nests, took the occasional egg and took it home. I suppose eventually they all got lost. It was a minor thing of egg collecting.

Brooklands Road, looking toward Bletchley Road. It hadn't really changed very much by Jack's time. His home, number 14, would be just off to the front left in this picture.

I played mainly with other children, rather than my brothers and sister. There was a two-year gap between us all. I used to play with the children next door and others in the street. We all knew what time we had to be in.

At Easter time we would go to the woods and pick primroses. On Good Friday Mother would give us a bottle of water or pop and some sandwiches. We would walk perhaps two miles to the woods, pick the primroses and other flowers, and bring them home. There were a lot of primroses growing then. I don't know if those woods are still there or not now.

I didn't have to be in when my father came home from work because he worked shifts. For the early morning shift there were callboys to wake him up. They came round and knocked on the door, waited until the man of the house, Dad, answered and then away they would go to the next one.

There was no electric light then, gas if you were lucky. The boys were employed as callboys by the railway to make sure the men got to work on time. The callboys' next job for the railway, if they progressed, was cleaning engines. From cleaners they could go to learn to be firemen and from firemen to be drivers.

My father started work in the railway sheds when he left school at fourteen. His parents had by then moved to Barton, about four miles from Cambridge. He had to walk the four miles to work and be there by 6 o'clock in the morning, then walk the four miles back in the evening.

Asked if the walk could be dangerous on dark mornings and

evenings, this was my father's reply:

There weren't any cars to run you over - might have been a horse go down the road.

About the callboys: two of them actually, and it's recorded in a book about the railways and Bletchley (*Bletchley Voices, Robert Cook*). The two callboys met eventually, after they'd been round, outside our house.

They couldn't remember which house was my father's. But my father was awake and he heard these boys arguing. One of them said, "Oh let the old bugger sleep then." So of course father got up and the boys were in real trouble when they got to work.

Just a few anecdotes about us.

There was a tradition of boys following in their father's footsteps, because there was quite a limit on what good jobs were available. At Bletchley it was mainly the brickworks or the railway.

Bletchley Station in the 1930s
Entrance and station yard to the front.

There was a job going at Wolverton, which was about 6 miles from Bletchley. There was a big carriage works at Wolverton, and the gas supplies and all that were supplied by the railway company, who built all these carriages for the main lines and everything.

I wanted a job with the gas and it would have involved in the first place cleaning gas cookers and all that kind of labouring.

I had to go to Rugby to be examined, to see whether I was fit. And I had to pass the same eyesight test as my father had for driving trains - and I failed!

After questions from the interviewer:

My father had worked his way up. Driver was the top job but there were various grades of train driver. If you were on the mainline, that's the expresses, then you were probably a bit better than on the local. My father worked on the main line, London to Bletchley (*as a first-class train driver*).

If my father could avoid it, he wouldn't work on a Sunday. Sometimes he had to but not if he could avoid it.

Answering another question:

Did we eat Sunday lunch as a family? Dinner - no such thing as lunch then! Or if you had lunch it was about 10 o'clock, a snack. We all sat round the table for dinner. Dinner was vegetables, whatever meat was available, good old solid puddings. Mother was a good cook.

None of us followed in my father's footsteps. My brothers studied and got good jobs. My brother Don in Canada, he'll be 93 this year, studied, burned all the midnight oil, learning about the gas. He worked for the Bletchley Gas Company. Then eventually in Vancouver, in British Columbia, he finished up as Sales Director of the Inland Natural Gas Company.

Another brother (*Bob*) studied, and he became Secretary of the Cooperative Society. My sister went into service, but not to sleep in. My next brother (*Bernard*) went into the Diplomatic Wireless Service and I was the odd one out.

I did study a bit at the Evening Institute and things like that but I didn't get that big job. I was too idle!

My sister had opportunities to study. Margaret was no slouch and she was a very good athlete. But there weren't the vacancies and everything for girls in those days, at least not so much; well, very little really.

Girls worked as skivvies, in service, and got married.

I don't suppose Margaret wanted to be a teacher like mother. She was quite up to things, as I say no slouch. She was a strong character, had to be with seven brothers around.

We all had to help mother in the house. I certainly did. I had to do quite a bit of housework, cleaning the floors. We had no carpets in those days. We had lino on the floor and it all had to be scrubbed and things like that.

I think the boys probably did more but memory doesn't really cover that bit of it. You didn't think of those sorts of things really, those days.

Boys had to do their share. It was fair and we were all family. And I still "keep" family, all family.

Asked about how he came to work at the brickworks, Dad said:

Those days it was still the depression and if you could get a reasonable job you were lucky. I thought I was, just as an office boy.

In those days there were no internal phones and no modern phones in the brickworks. Being the office boy, if the works manager was out in the works and was wanted on the (*external*) telephone it was, "Jack, go and find Mr Hersey."

And wherever he was, it didn't matter; whatever the weather, Jack had to go and find Mr Hersey.

The brickworks in 1928, with the knothole (claypit), front left.

The term knothole seemingly came from the knots, or lumps, of clay that were dug out of the pit.

How long was I office boy? About three years I suppose and then the office enlarged...

An interruption brought the question of wages.

My first wage was fifteen shillings (*15/-*) a week. It wasn't a lot of money. What did I do with it? Gave my mother most of it! It was expected. We all contributed to the house. I probably gave her ten shillings of it.

I first started work at thirteen. As a boy, I used to get up very early in the morning and do a paper round. I went to school, and in the evening and on Saturdays I went to work for a wine and spirit merchant, delivering orders and bottling wine.

Between the newsagent and the wine and spirit merchant I got fifteen shillings a week when I was thirteen. But I never did any sport. I hadn't time for sport!

At that time there was just one wine and spirit shop, Mr Staniford, who I worked for. He would have wine come in these - 60 gallon or whatever they were - big barrels. He would put them on a stillion, which is where the barrels go, even the beer barrels.

He paid a penny for returned bottles. We would see that they were clean and then wash them. And I would sit and bottle, put the corks in, put the caps on, and everything.

I made deliveries but in comparison to today, the wine sales were minimal. It was mostly red wine but I've no idea where it came from. It could have been Italy or Portugal or anywhere. That sort of thing didn't interest me. I don't know what a bottle cost. I did taste it as I was allowed to have a little, a small glass, not much.

Next door to the wine and spirit merchant was a banana ripening sheds. In the school holidays I would sometimes go there in the afternoons, hang there (*sic*) and eat bananas. But when I did that, I got boils. So I had to stop eating bananas. I always think it was a combination of having a little bit of wine **and** the bananas!

I can eat bananas now but I seldom eat any fruit. I do have wine with my dinner every day.

Growing up in the depression was normal for us. But when I started as office boy, before I got to the brickworks every morning there would be a queue of men wanting a job.

The foreman would go out and he would say to the men, "I'll have you, you and you." Then he would actually say, "And the rest of you can bugger off!"

I did feel lucky to have work. There was a job advertisement and I think my father got it for me actually. I had an interview with the works manager and got started. I had about two miles to bike to work. I progressed to wages clerk, did that for about three years and then war came. 15th September 1939 I had to join the army.

Before the war broke out the government had started to call young people up for what they called the militia and I was in the second batch of the militia.

I'd had to go to Bedford to pass my medical exam and so on. I should have done six months' training but instead of that I did six and a half years in the war.

I was called up and went to join the Royal Army Medical Corps. I finished three months' training at the middle of December and went on a week's leave to home, went back and then went to France. I joined a unit (*3rd Casualty Clearing Station*) and stayed with that unit all through the war.

WARTIME

We went to Mondicourt, a village between Arras and Amiens. That was the phony (*sic*) war.

It was a very, very cold winter, terrible cold winter. We stayed in an old building, no heating and I can't remember any windows. We had two blankets each and I had a stretcher to sleep on.

Eventually we went into the village. We used to take washing and so on, take some soap and take some food - whatever we had to pay for the washing.

I managed to get an eiderdown then. Otherwise all through the winter, night and day, I kept all my clothes on. I never took my clothes off, except for a wash. There was deep snow and it was very, very cold there.

Then as the proper war broke out, we moved up further towards Belgium (*Mont des Cats and De Panne*), and eventually to Dunkirk. I came out of Dunkirk May the 31st, and arrived home.

We thought - or rather I thought, because I was on my own...

My unit sergeant gave me a pack of medical records to carry and said, "We'll help you on the way," but I didn't see any more of my unit at all. He said "You set off and we'll catch you up." Where they went, I don't know! They all got home.

I set off for Dunkirk. After passing Bray-Dunes and having got quite a way along the beach I saw a sailor, so I said, "Any chance of getting off?" He said, "You stay there tonight but you can't take that pack with you." So I left it on the beach.

At night time we went through the water up to our chests to get on to a light boat, because the water was very shallow at Dunkirk. It was warm. I got on to this other boat and I thought, "Well we shall be home in the morning." Then when I woke up we weren't.

The skipper of the boat wouldn't leave while he could see anybody. He cruised along the shore all night.

The last man brought on to our boat had been shot through with machine gun bullets and he died within sight of England. The Germans were very close behind us at Dunkirk.

Then we spent a time in England, going to different places...

Interrupted by the interviewer with a question on his unit:

We were a Casualty Clearing Station and the Casualty Clearing Station was the first unit down the line, with operating theatres and so on. We took the casualties then and what could be operated on there were done, the others evacuated to a general hospital as fast as possible. Yes, I saw some gory sights, but they had to pass on.

In December 1941 we were intending to go to the Far East but we didn't get there. We stopped at Sierra Leone. I always remember where I was at Christmas, and Christmas morning we were there.

Then we went to Cape Town, South Africa, for four days. There I was able to go and visit people I'd been given the address for.

The South Africans were wonderful people. If soldiers were stood looking in windows or something down the road they were asked if they wanted to go home with the civilians.

Next we went up the Indian Ocean, Suez Canal, and then up into the Middle East. I went as far as Beirut, lovely place then.

In Beirut, friend on the left

Then we came back down to Cairo and there, although I was only there four hours - I don't know how it was arranged - met my brother Bernard. He was in the RAF.

He had already been up as far as Benghazi and then driven back. So we had four hours together.

Brother Bernard on the left

Then we went up the desert with the 8th Army and right through there (*including Tobruk, Benghazi and El Alamein*). I had another brother, Henry, there in the RAF.

And it was a very funny thing because Bernard met Henry, they were at Heliopolis, the RAF place. But Bernard was walking up the road and Henry was coming down under escort. I don't know what he'd done, but he was under escort. And that's how they met in Egypt. They couldn't talk to one another then but they met together after that.

Then we went to Malta for a rest, then the invasion of Sicily, then up into Italy.

The interviewer asked Dad if he had ever been in danger during the war! He seemed stunned for a few moments and then gave this example - all that came to mind at the time, I think:

When we were coming in to land in Italy, we came under fire from the German guns on the coast. We really thought one of the shells was going to hit our ship. They came very, very close.

And then when we finished our service there we came home, again on a troop ship at Christmas, in December 1943.

We had a half ration of bully beef for Christmas dinner. We got home and I went to Cambridge. After five months in England, we went on to the invasion of Normandy.

Interviewer asks about his work and those he cared for:

We cared for the injured, the casualties. But you got times when you came out of battle and then cared for the sick.

There were two casualty clearing stations to a Corps. In battle you took all the casualties and you shipped them back.

We went through as far as Nijmegen and then to Arnhem. We went up there with the Guards Armoured Division to Nijmegen, and got cut off for four days. We spent a time there and then we went up to the Ardennes for the Battle of the Bulge.

After that we came back to Nijmegen for the last battle, the Battle of the Rhine, and into Germany and through, and ended up at Hanover.

Surprisingly, I lost no friends.

We had two nursing sisters who were wounded just after the landing. People didn't realise the sisters went in with us and when we got shelled one night, two night sisters got wounded badly enough to get them out. The army medical people moved us then to another site out of the way.

On D-Day we were in convoy going to the invasion, and we were just off Dover when the big guns opened up and they hit the ship in front of us.

If it had been in a few more hundred yards it would have been us but we were lucky.

M.T. 2. on fire off Dover after being hit by a shell from German long range guns at 13.05 Hrs. 6th June 1944.

Jack's grandson Winn had the original photo, with the negative and a copy of my father's description, mounted and framed professionally. They have now been passed down to Jack's eldest great grandson, Luke.

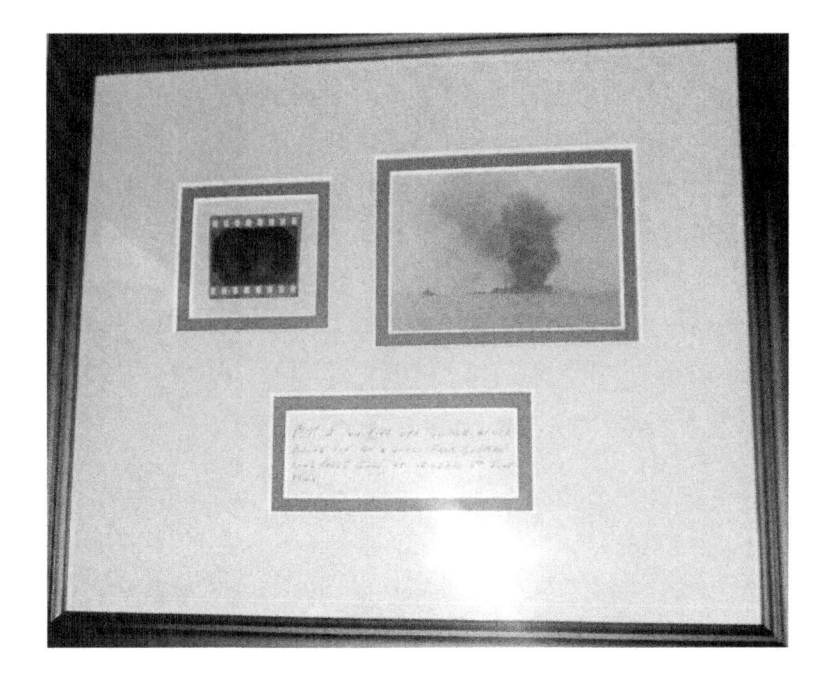

After we landed at Normandy (*Gold Beach*) we set up our hospital. But the space was so limited they built an airstrip just behind us.

The big guns used to fire, go over us all the time, even at night when you were laying on the ground because you didn't have anything else to lay on. Every time the big guns fired, you went, "boomf, boomf." (*sic*).

That was the sort of life but it was there and you just did it. You didn't know where you were going or what you were doing until somebody said... whatever. And then you went.

I got out, came home alright. I got home for the very odd time in between but I was away for five Christmases.

Dad acknowledged to the interviewer that he was very relieved when the war ended. And yes, he'd had enough after 6½ years.

POSTWAR

BLETCHLEY

When I came back, Bletchley was about the same. It hadn't been bombed. I think there'd just been a bomb dropped further down the line, trying to hit the station.

My job was still there as they had to keep your jobs open. But things at the brickworks changed then. There was a boom in the building trade. And I was now in the Personnel Department.

The first people we tried to employ were from Glasgow, Liverpool and Belfast. We would have train loads come in. We used to document all these people. In the morning they had a pound (*British sterling*) and a night at the hostel. They'd had a day's travel that didn't cost them anything. And in the morning, if you'd got two left to work you were lucky!

Then we employed Polish servicemen. They were still in the army and they eventually went off to places like the mills in Lancashire.

We had the European Voluntary Workers and then I think it was the Italians next. I used to document them all and put them in the hostel. The personnel managers and people went out to Italy and recruited them.

When the building trade was depressed, as happens from time to time, the Italians left for other jobs. That was how we came with the Indians and Pakistanis, now all round. They came and then they brought their families. I don't know what the contracts were as I had nothing to do with that. I only took them on and documented them and then they would go to the works or whatever.

Before the war, the brick company used to have big Sports Days at Stewartby and at Peterborough. I went to Peterborough cycle racing and won two or three prizes. But after the war that sort of thing started off as Sports Days, but only local, and then went to Family Days. Then there was no interest and there aren't any now.

The head office of the London Brick Company used to be in Africa House in London, then another locality near Madame Tussaud's, and then it moved to Stewartby

STEWARTBY

I came here (*to Stewartby*) to organise a Sports Day and then from 1954 I was employed as Secretary of the Social and Sports Association.

A Sports Day at Stewartby

There was a Club, and we had about two thousand employee members here. There were about ten different sports sections: angling, badminton, I can't remember them all now.

We paid tuppence (*two old pence*) a week to belong to the Social and Sports (*Club*) and the company paid a penny a week for every tuppence. We had committees to run things but sections had their own committees. They were subsidised to a certain extent.

At Christmas time it was very busy. We used to have indoor games of all sorts in the Club. We used to put a big sheet up on the wall for results and had a big Finals Night.

Then we started the Old Folks and Widows Party in 1955, when I was here. There were many more widows than men, or than married couples - there always are.

We used to lay on a big meal for them, entertainment, give them money. The ladies also got a box of chocolates the men a small bottle of whisky.

We used to have about six hundred children for children's parties, a big Whist Drive every year with about two hundred people. And so we had a terrific, busy Christmas here.

My job was to organise all that, though not the sections themselves. There were too many. I was on my own in the office, didn't have an assistant at that time though I did eventually.

Over the years the sections fizzled out. People didn't want to do the work. Often if somebody would do the donkey work people would play, but they didn't want to do any part of the organisation. So eventually they nearly all went.

We used to have at one time seven Associations, different Clubs: Peterborough, Arlesey, Bletchley, Calvert, all over.

We had a Social and Sports Council. Then eventually I became Secretary to the Social and Sports Council and had an assistant.

I terminated my employment in 1981. I applied for redundancy because they were wanting to reduce staff and I'd had just about enough. I did just over 48 years with the company.

We had a house in Stewartby, 199 Wavell Close.

The London Brick Company employed a team of groundsmen, who kept all the public areas of the village in pristine condition.

Front Door facing Wavell Close, taken in later years, when Hanson no longer employed groundsmen.

Early years: the left-hand windows of the building, facing Stewartby Way, belong to 199. The door and windows to the right belong to 200 Stewartby Way.

And then we moved here three years ago.

"Here" was a bungalow, 2 Sir Malcolm Stewart Homes.

The following picture shows it from the front.

In answer to a query about the move to Stewartby, whether Dad liked the change and it was for the better:

Well, it was something different. And you're always trying to get a little bit more money, more promotion. So yes, it was better to move here.

Kitty didn't like it so much, especially the first day we came to look at the house. It was raining, and we came on the train. (*It's a long walk from Stewartby Halt, as it was then, to the house.*)

But the company redecorated right through, from top to bottom. We just provided the wallpaper for the walls where we wanted it and they did the rest. They moved us and we got used to it.

It was work and home and the children, two girls who went to the school here. It was bit different then. And our eldest Jean (*born October 1944*) won a scholarship to the Bedford Girls High School, which is the best school in Bedford. Carole (*born February 1949*) won a scholarship to the Dame Alice School. So they did very well.

There we are, settled down in a nice bungalow with a nice view, no rent to pay, no TV licence - and two old codgers!

I have enjoyed my life here. No, I don't think about how different staying in Bletchley would have been. We don't like Bletchley much now; we don't go back.

When they did Milton Keynes, Bletchley went down. And then across the main road going out they built a great big black building, and altered it.

I don't go to Bletchley now. I can't make it as I used to and there's nobody of our generation living there. My sister-in-law who we used to go and see, she's in Milton Keynes hospital having had a stroke. And so I don't bother. My youngest brother lives at Winslow and my other brother of course lives in Canada.

In a sense this is now an idyllic place for us to live. It's our final home. We have a nice common room. We have a coffee morning, and there are whist drives and all sorts.

The brickworks has been very positive for the area, because of the employment. And the company built the village, built the school. In 1936 we'd got a swimming pool, a sports club, a village hall - and it's a lovely village hall.

Village Hall

The company did all that and there were all the sports facilities. It was basically nice. Work was hard and you got the old stinky smoke from the chimneys. I never minded that. I was brought up with it all my life.

But I know one thing. It's not nearly as bad as the smell from the tip, Shanks and McEwan's tip, that's awful when you get it.

Shanks and McEwan had the contract to use a nearby worked out knothole, for dumping waste as landfill.

There's another pit out here now with one desperate to obtain the rights of it and others wanting to stop the tipping. I think it would be awful. The prevailing wind is west to south west.

We have a big school here, getting bigger. I think about when the smells come and the children are in class or outside; it's awful.

There's one thing most of us old Stewartby people utterly dislike. The Stewarts had the school built in 1936. It was always Stewartby School, later became Stewartby Middle School.

Stewartby School

Then some "blasphemians" (*sic*) changed it to Marston Valley Middle School. I think that was awful. Why disturb the Stewarts' name when they did so much for this place? They built a school, supplied a school.

I don't know who made the decision to change it. I objected most strongly, as lots of people did. But the powers that be decided, and I suppose it cost a lot of money to do it because of changing all the stationery and everything else. They weren't satisfied that it was the Stewarts' school.

The Stewarts didn't just put their money away. They put it into houses and gardens and 86 bungalows here. They supplied their employees with a swimming pool and facilities to enjoy.

So why alter the name of the school? I don't think anybody can give me a reason *for* altering it.

Here the tape ends.

Stewartby swimming pool in its heyday. The brickworks canteen is the building to the left, at the shallow end of the pool.

JACK BLANE'S WAR

Remembrance Day 2003. A far cry from a war that is never forgotten.

Medals are - Top: 1939-45 Star, Africa Star with 8th Army Clasp, Italy Star, France-Germany Star, 1939-45 Campaign Medal.

Bottom: Dunkirk Veterans Medal, Normandy Medal. Worn with pride.
Following is the account my father wrote of "his"' war, in his own words.

He wrote it in 2002 at the age of 83, for the family and especially his grandchildren.

No 7266456, Private J Blane Royal Army Medical Corps
No 3 (BR) Casualty Clearing Station

Later Lance Corporal he refused promotion to Sgt, as it would have meant leaving his unit and being re-assigned, probably to Burma.

I entered military service at Crookham Barracks, 15th September 1939. After three months' training I had Embarkation Leave for one week at Christmas.

Having embarked for France on a bitterly cold New Year's Eve, I was sent to Number 3 Casualty Clearing Station (3 CCS) at Mondicourt and remained with that unit throughout the war.

It was very cold, with deep snow. I read last year, 2001, that 1940 was the coldest winter since 1815.

I only had a stretcher to sleep on and two blankets, in a cold, old house with no heating. For two months I went to bed with all my clothes on, including my greatcoat and gas cape.

When the "Phony War" ended and Germany invaded, we gradually made our way to the coast.

We had some dodgy times on the way, including evacuating a clearly marked ambulance train of severely burned civilians from Rotterdam, whilst under attack from German planes.

On 31st May we were ordered to leave our billet for hopeful evacuation. My sergeant gave me a big pack of medical record books, then told me to set off to Dunkirk and that on the way the others would help me.

I set off into France and kept plodding along the sand.

I did not see any more members of our unit but finally saw a Royal Navy man. I asked him if there was any chance of getting off.

He told me to stay where I was and wait but that I could not take the pack. So I just threw it down and left it on the beach.

I seemed to be alone and must have fallen asleep. When it became dark a lot of other troops assembled and a smallish boat arrived.

We had to wade into the sea up to our chests. The Navy chap in charge said that when he ordered, "Stop," we had to stop trying to get aboard or he would shoot us - and I am sure that he would have.

We were all finally taken to a larger "little ship." I thought, "Oh, good: we should be in England by morning."

When I woke up, big shock. We were still cruising off shore and the skipper would not leave while he could see anyone on the beach.

The last man to be brought aboard was in a bad way, having been shot by a machine gun. He died within sight of England.

After disembarking I was put on a train and eventually arrived at Oswestry Barracks about midnight, still soaked through.

I had one nightmare after this while I was billeted with nice people in Leeds, where I finally rejoined my unit all safe and sound.

From June 1940 to December 1941 I was stationed at various places in England.

Kitty and I married on 9th October 1940. That Christmas was the last we had together until 1945.

Our unit left Liverpool in December 1941 and we spent Christmas Day that year in Sierra Leone harbour.

Later, I had four lovely days with civilian friends in Cape Town, South Africa.

We then went to Palestine and to Beirut, which was a lovely place then.

On our way to the 8th Army I met up with my brother Bernard for four hours in Cairo. I never did know how that was arranged or by whom.

I spent Christmas 1942 at Tobruk and New Year's Eve at Benghazi. Then it was on to the last battle for the 8th Army in North Africa *(El Alamein)*.

After that, we went to Malta for two weeks' rest and then it was the invasion of Sicily and into Southern Italy.

Our ship came under heavy fire while we lay off Italy prior to landing.

We sailed for England from Bari on a lousy, overcrammed ship. We had half a ration of bully beef for Christmas dinner 1943. At night all the floors, the dining tables and hammocks, were full of men.

In January 1944 I arrived in England and was stationed in Cambridge, hooray!! I was allowed a sleeping out pass. Kitty came to Cambridge and we had a lovely time, staying with my Aunt Alice.

On D-Day, 6th June, we sailed in convoy down the Thames. Once off Dover we could see and hear the big German guns in Calais firing across the Channel.

They hit the ship directly ahead of us, setting it on fire. It was terrible to see. How lucky we were to escape unharmed.

We lay off the French coast until D-Day plus two. Then we landed on Gold Beach with 30 Corps and set up our Casualty Clearing Station.

We were very busy and it was very noisy from the gunfire. I slept in a ditch. The Germans shelled us one night and two Nursing Sisters were injured. The army moved us to a safer area the next day.

On we went to Brussels and then to Eindhoven. Next it was Nijmegen where the road back (our supply road) was cut off by the Germans for four days.

We took casualties from the battle for Arnhem. Six operating theatres were working, three on day shift and three on night shift. I did not leave the hospital building for two weeks.

After two months there we were relieved by the Canadians.

Christmas Day 1944 was spent somewhere in Belgium. Then it was on to the Ardennes and the "Battle of the Bulge" to help the Americans, who suffered heavy losses.

There was deep snow and it was bitterly, bitterly cold.

We were back to Nijmegen for the Battle for the Rhine. Twentyfive pounder guns fired over the hospital all day. The forest flooded too and all casualties and equipment were wet through.

I had a short home leave in March, to see Kitty and meet my new daughter for the first time. Then it was back to my unit.

We made our way into Germany where, after being in various places, we ended up just outside Hanover.

December 1945 and back in England. I had four weeks demob leave. So Christmas 1945 I was home at last. Demobbed February 1946.

There were Good Times and Bad Times - but always Good Friends.

Jack Blane

3rd March 2002

RAMC Reference **Number: 211042**

I, and all our family, are very proud of my father.

JACK BLANE ADDS TO WARTIME MEMORIES

Told some years ago, mainly during late night conversations with me and after a whisky or two.

On New Year's Day 1940 we disembarked to cliffs at Dieppe. There were two men to a tent and we each had two blankets and a groundsheet. Although it was against regulations we doubled up at night without undressing. It was just too cold and we had a lot of snow.

We were collected and went to 3rd Casualty Clearing Station, with them to Mondicourt, and on to Pars. There we were billeted in a house. We had a foot of snow and it was freezing.

We went into the village and thought we were asking, in French, for a blanket. What were we given? Jam! We did eventually get a quilt.

While we were there I had a chest infection, probably bronchitis. An old lady put a mustard plaster on my chest to treat it. Next day we marched all day in full kit. I was sweating but I was cured!

We moved on to near Cassel and then the Germans began their real push. We made rounds at night, after being on duty in the day. The tents that were our wards covered a large area. We were followed by gleaming eyes on our rounds - local dogs.

Again, after a full day on duty I would have night calls to CSM (meningitis) cases, having to hold them down raving. We had very little in the way of medicines.

The first real casualty I saw in France was in a chateau, where we opened the door and saw a man lying with his brains hanging out but still alive. We closed the door and left. It was too much, too awful.

We took burns casualties from a Red Cross train, machine gunned by the Germans as we were evacuating. I had four in my care in the ambulance, all children.

Machine guns continued firing. We captured two Germans and our officer had to be restrained from shooting them.

I'm not sure what the next town was (*from writing on the back of an old photo I discovered it was De Panne in Belgium*), where we were put up in the Hotel Splendide - on a concrete floor in the hotel garage!

From there we were evacuated to Dunkirk. Separated from my unit I walked along the beach until I got there.

The beach at Dunkirk was a terrible sight. We were taken off at night. I had to off-load our medical records, which I had carried all the way.

My gas mask was coming off so I jettisoned that too. Waiting to be taken on board ship we were up to our necks in fluorescent water.

Even when I was getting on board, a sailor with a gun said he would shoot us if we didn't obey him. I believe he would have.

I was never dry until well after arrival in the UK. (*What must that have been like for the men?*) I was still in wet clothes when I got to Oswestry.

Next morning we were not in England but still circling round Dunkirk. We took on a chap riddled with machine gun bullets. The captain sent down a pint of rum for the casualty. He could not drink it, was in a very bad way, had lost so much blood, awful.

So while we looked after him as best we could, a mate and I drank it - with no noticeable effects, despite having been on half rations for a week. The casualty died in sight of the English coast.

When we travelled by ship around Africa to get to Egypt, the sea was terribly rough in the Bay of Biscay. Most of the men stayed in their hammocks or hanging over the ship's rail! For some reason, it didn't affect me at all. Since hardly anyone else wanted their breakfast, I had plenty.

We had to keep our uniforms on all through the voyage, night and day. They were made from army serge and the trousers chafed the inside of my thighs dreadfully. The raw areas got infected, very painful, and I still have the scars.

Moving through Europe after D-Day, we simply got used to passing bins filled with amputated arms and legs in the mornings on our way to breakfast.

Understated, restrained, but among the memories that never left him.

Lighter memories.

In Beirut one evening, a few of us were looking for somewhere to get a beer. Some Aussies told us they knew of a place and took us there. It was up an outside staircase and turned out to be a brothel! We were a bit taken aback. But you could get a beer there, so we stayed drinking for a few hours.

When we left, I was rather the worse for wear and fell down the steps. That didn't do me a lot of good. I was taken to my own hospital, though thankfully not badly hurt. But it took me a good while to live that down.

In North Africa I caught sandfly fever and that also put me out of action for a short time.

I was never wounded but after we'd made our way into Germany I was hospitalised with bronchitis. That's when I made the stuffed elephant.

Made for me, I remember the toy. The elephant had a navy blue felt body with orange blanket stitch edging. I don't know how Dad managed to stuff the very thin, ivory coloured tusks.

What follows in this chapter is taken from other memories. Some I was told by Dad and some come from other family members.

Dad spoke warmly of the ANZACS with whom his unit had been stationed in both North Africa and Italy. He kept up correspondence with one of them, with whom he had become good friends, for quite some time after the war.

When we were living at Whiteley Crescent, so it would be around 1950, this friend - whom I knew only as Uncle Bill, visited England and came to stay with us. It frustrates me now that I didn't learn more.

This next story is one that I remember hearing from both Dad and various other family members. Sadly, I'm afraid the finer details are a bit hazy to me at this remove.

Mum's family was from Beighton, a small mining village near Sheffield, where most still lived. Her sister Annie and brother-in-law Arthur had converted the front room of their house into a small newsagent's shop, though Arthur still also worked in the local coal mine.

Coal mining was a reserved occupation, meaning that miners did not get called to serve in the armed forces. Coal was a very much needed fuel.

In December 1940 while Dad was in England, following his return from Dunkirk and prior to leaving for North Africa, he was stationed at an army camp not far from Beighton. He took some leave, which he and Mum spent with Annie and Arthur.

The newspapers were delivered to the customers' homes by paper boys. Uncle Arthur walked round the village once a week to collect the money for the papers.

Shortly before this Christmas, Dad and Mum's brother Tom went with him on his collection. At just about every house where they called they were offered - and took - an alcoholic drink.

After finishing the round they had to pick up a ham for Aunt Annie from the butcher's shop, which was on a bus route that ran through the village. When they had collected the ham they caught a bus home, climbing to the top deck (where they could smoke) with their purchase. When they came to their stop, off they got - but without the ham! They didn't realise they had left it on the bus when they alighted.

When they walked into the house, of course Annie asked where the ham was - and oh dear, she wasn't at all happy and let them know it. They rather got the rough edge or her tongue.

So out they went to wait at the bus stop on the other side of the road, for the bus to make its return journey. Fortunately, their bus journey had been outward bound. Now the bus was headed back to the depot, with the ham still on board for them to retrieve - to great relief.

Next morning, Dad had to return to his barracks. He told us that he groped his way along the wall to the gate! I suspect that may have been somewhat of an exaggeration. However, not normally being a heavy drinker, he was clearly rather the worse for wear.

As for Tom, he was usually more straitlaced, he and his wife Edna distancing themselves from the rest of the family as time went by. But he enjoyed himself that afternoon, even if Edna disapproved.

IMAGES

We applied for a Dunkirk medal for Dad, which duly arrived and which he wore with pride when at last he wore his other medals, so many years after the war.

He was also awarded a certificate from the town of Dunkirk and was a member of the Dunkirk Veterans Association, as you see.

LA VILLE DE DUNKERQUE

à *Jack Blane*
Royal Army Medical Corps

En mémoire des Combats de Mai et Juin 1940

Association Nationale des A. C.
de Flandres-Dunkerque 40

Le Maire,
CLAUDE PROUVOYEUR
1940
Dunkirk Veterans Association

Amicale des Anciens de
Marine Dunkerque

LIVRE D'OR N° 24056

Certificate of recognition from the town of Dunkirk.

Jean Blane Flannery

1940
Dunkirk Veterans Association
INTERNATIONAL HEADQUARTERS
LEEDS
Registered under War Charities Act, 1940
Patron
THE MAYOR OF DUNKIRK

AIMS
1. To assist all needy members and their families
2. To foster the spirit of comradeship which existed on and off the beaches of Dunkirk 1940

Branch _BEDFORD_
Member's Name _J. BLANE_
Address _199 WATERS CLOSE_
STEWARTBY
BEDS

Date of Joining _____

Membership No. _104_
LIFE MEMBER/~~ORDINARY MEMBER/ASSOC.~~ MEMBER
Please indicate Type of Membership

SUBSCRIPTIONS
Subscriptions are due on the 1st January each year
Please send your card or quote membership Number when paying subscriptions
Please advise your Branch Secretary if you change your address

1940
Dunkirk Veterans Association

MEMBERSHIP CARD

Jack Blane

Certificate
1940   2000

The Province of West Flanders, Belgium
to veteran Pte. J. Blane No 3 C.C.S. RAMC

This certificate of 'Pilgrimage' is given
to commemorate the 60th anniversary of the evacuation
of British & Allied Forces from the beaches of
De Panne in May/June 1940, and the final
Pilgrimage of the 1940 Dunkirk Veterans' Association
on 5 June 2000.

Paul BREYNE
Governor of the Province

5 June 2000

60 Year Commemoration

At the end of the war and before Dad's discharge there was a thanksgiving service for the successful end to the war in Europe. I don't know if Dad attended but he had, and kept, a copy of the service booklet, despite having lost all faith in a loving God after his wartime experiences.

Front of Service Booklet

No. 7266456 4c.i. J. Blane. R.A.M.C.
Called up for Military Service
15" Sept. 1939

3rd (British) Casualty Clearing Station
January 1940 to February 1946

Evacuated Dunkirk
Invasion of Sicily
Invasion of Normandy

Demobbed February 1946.

Jean Blane Flannery

SECOND ARMY

𝕿𝖍𝖆𝖓𝖐𝖘𝖌𝖎𝖛𝖎𝖓𝖌 𝕾𝖊𝖗𝖛𝖎𝖈𝖊

ON CONCLUSION

OF

THE CAMPAIGN IN NORTH WEST EUROPE

6TH JUNE, 1944 TO 5TH MAY, 1945

Page 2

THE PATH OF THE ARMY

1944

JUNE	6th	. . .	The Assault - NORMANDY ✓
	27th	. . .	The ODON
JULY	9th	. . .	CAEN
	29th	. . .	CAUMONT ✓
AUGUST	7th	. . .	MONT PINCON ✓
	20th	. . .	FALAISE ✓
	25th	. . .	The SEINE ✓
SEPTEMBER	2nd	. . .	The SOMME ✓
	3rd	. . .	BRUSSELS ✓
	4th	. . .	ANTWERP ✓
	3rd - 11th	.	The Canals - ALBERT and ESCAUT
	17th	. . .	ARNHEM NIJMEGEN
	17th - 29th	.	The Rivers - MAAS and WAAL
OCTOBER	22nd - 27th	.	'S HERTOGENBOSCH - TILBURG
NOV. 14th - DEC. 13th		.	The Rivers - MAAS and ROER
DECEMBER	21st	. . .	The ARDENNES ✓

1945

JANUARY	13th	. . .	SITTARD *Nov-Dec 1944*
MARCH	24th	. . .	The RHINE ✓
APRIL	5th	. . .	The WESER ✓
	26th	. . .	BREMEN
	29th	. . .	The ELBE
MAY	2nd	. . .	The BALTIC
April	*25th*		*VERDEN — FINIS.*

From the landing on Gold Beach to the final destination in Germany, Dad ticked off his campaigns and as you see added Nijmegen to Arnhem. Both were terrible.

National Anthem

God save our gracious King,
Long live our noble King,
God save the King;
Send him victorious,
Happy and glorious,
Long to reign over us;
God save the King.

Then shall the Chaplain say

Lord, at the close of this campaign, we meet together before Thee to pour out our hearts in fervent thanksgiving for all Thy loving kindness to us during the long days of battle, and to dedicate ourselves afresh to the service of Thy Kingdom. We desire to thank Thee for the deliverance from the hand of our enemies; for the devotion, even unto death, of our comrades who have fallen in the fight; and for all the willing sacrifices made in Thy Cause. Grant to us, Lord, who have been preserved amid so many dangers, a due sense of all Thy mercies, that we may be unfeignedly thankful, and serve Thee faithfully all the days of our life.

Amen.

Page 4

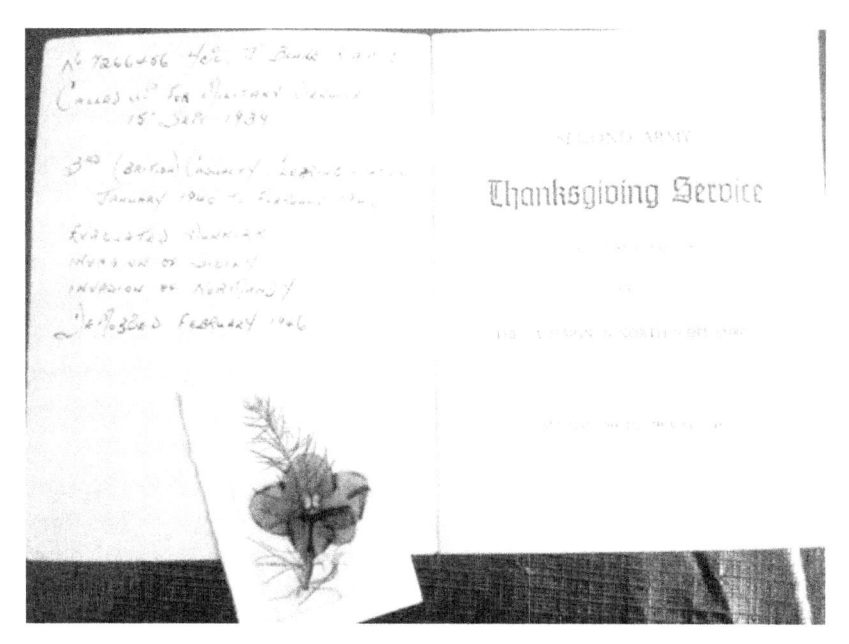

We believe that the pressed flower, found in the service booklet, is an African Violet - perhaps sent to his darling Kitty from South Africa?

The two faces of the XXX Corps commemorative medallion, still treasured along with all memorabilia.

Some are within my branch of the family, some my sister's.

GRANDFATHER ALTERED OUR NAME
(We lost an I and gained an E)

A few years ago Cousin Freda sent me a copy of her information on the Blane Family Tree. This chart stirred my interest and sent me on a number of visits to the Bedford Library in Harpur Street and to the Count Records Department in County Hall, Bedford. The librarians in both places were most helpful to my uncertain requests and I am most grateful to them for their assistance.

From the library I obtained, in addition to other material, a Photostat copy (cost 10p) of the Mormon's church records from 1600-1785 of the Families Blain, Blayne, Blane, Blayns and Blaine.

The records covered fourteen towns and villages, mostly in Cambridgeshire, but strangely none in Sandy, although there were Blain's living in sandy in 1769 (see below).

The librarian did inform me that not all churches would allow the Mormons access to their records. During those 185 years Meldreth had 17 Blayne's, 13 Blane's and 14 Blaine's. Croxton had 18, all Blane's, of which the most unusual Christian name was 'Tubal Cain' (Genesis 4:22), son of Mary Howard 1st Feb 1750.

In the County Records Department I was able to copy the 1851 Census for Girtford and Sandy, also the Sandy Baptisms covering 1821-1850.

The Census shows that my Great Grandparents William and Mary Blain were 42 years of age and lived at 22 Girtford. Great Grandfather was born in Sandy, his wife in nearby Hatch. They had six children, of whom five were recorded, including Grandfather Charles, born 1845.

Also in the Census are another Blain family, Thomas and Ann, both born in Sandy in 1769 and living at 17 Girtford. I have to wonder if they were my Great, Great Grandparents.

The Sandy Baptisms 1841-1850 records that Grandfather Charles Blain was baptised on 11th May 1845 by the Rev H Cooke, who spelled his name as Blaine.

During 1841-1850 the Rev Cooke baptised ten Blain or Blaine children. Seven of these were spelled Blain, including Grandfather's sister Eliza 1841 and Susan 1848.

The Sandy Baptisms from 1821-1850 records twenty Blain or Blaine children and it would appear to depend on the rector whether an e was added to Blain. The Revd Cooke baptised nineteen of the twenty and Revd L Lamporn baptised Grandfather's brother Joseph on 17th July 1836 and recorded him as Blaine.

I recently examined my parents' marriage certificate and discovered that it was Grandfather who changed our family name to Blane.

Father is recorded as Charles Blane and Grandfather and his wife Jane both signed their names as Blane.

Mystery solved? Why Grandfather, born Blain, baptised Blaine, changed the spelling to Blane, I shall never know!

Jack Blane
16th November 1995

NOTES ON THE BLANE FAMILY HISTORY

Great Grandfather William Blain married Mary Miles (both born 1809). They had six children - William 1829, Joseph 1835, Elizabeth 1838, Eliza 1841 (who married a Feltwell), our Grandfather Charles 1845 and Susan 1848.

Grandfather Charles Blain, born at Sandy, was a platelayer on the railway. He married Jane Twinn (born 1846) from Duxford, Cambs.

They had seven children - Henry William 1869, Arthur John 1872, Jane 1875, Bessie 1878, Charles (our father) 1880, Alice 1883 and Eliza 1886. Charles and Jane died at Barton and were buried in the churchyard.

Grandfather Henry Norman Powell, born 1856, became a ship's steward. His father was Thomas Powell, who was a Master Builder.

Grandmother Mary (*inserted*) Elizabeth Miller, born 18th August 1856, was the daughter of John Miller, who was a miller by trade. (*We've discovered she was in fact simply Elizabeth Miller, born 15 June 1855.*)

Henry Norman Powell and Mary Elizabeth Miller were married in St Thomas' Church, Stepney, Middx, on 15th April 1877. The witnesses named on their marriage certificate were George and Francis Clara Conalley (*sic*) Presumably neither of their parents was present. Henry lived at 7 Redmans Road and Elizabeth at 1 Canal Road, both in Stepney.

Soon after their marriage they moved to Rotherhithe where our mother May Elizabeth Margaret Fraser Powell was born, 15th July

1878. Later they moved to 46 Park Street, Aylesbury, Bucks.

He left his wife Elizabeth and is believed to have settled in San Antonio, Texas, USA. He died in the early part of this century but details are not known. Yet according to the Aylesbury Cemetery register Elizabeth was a widow when she died 20th October 1899. *(See Appendix)*

Elizabeth was Matron of HM Convict Prison (Women's), Aylesbury. She became ill and died in the prison hospital of peritonitis on Friday 20th October 1899. Her body was interred in Aylesbury cemetery and the funeral service conducted by the Revd J Knight Newton, 25th October 1899.

Father Charles Henry Blane was born at Haslingfield, Cambs, 11th July 1880. He died at 14 Broooklands Road, Bletchley, Bucks, 26th Jan 1956, of chronic myeloid leukaemia and was cremated at Milton, near Northampton. His ashes were deposited in the rose garden of the crematorium (as were Mother's, later).

When Dad started work on the railway he had to walk from Barton to Cambridge (about 4 miles) and back each day. He was in the locomotive department of the railway and progressed to a fireman on the footplate (all engines were fired by coal then).

His work probably took him to Aylesbury (there was a branch line from Cheddington), where he met and married our mother. Father later became a First Class Driver and retired at the age of 65.

Mother, May Elizabeth Margaret Fraser Powell was born 15th July 1878 at Rotherhithe, London. She died at Renny Lodge, Newport Pagnell, Bucks, 1st June 1971.

Mother went to school in Paradise Street, Rotherhithe. She became a school teacher after serving four years apprenticeship in the Christ Church National Infant School, ending in January 1897.

She was Assistant Mistress in the Hampden National School (Great and Little Hampden, Bucks), from 13th September 1897 to 13th September 1898. There is no further record until she married in 1904.

Mother and Father married in Aylesbury Parish Church, 15th February 1904. At that time they both lived at 46 Park Street, Aylesbury. The witnesses to the marriage were Dad's parents, Charles and Jane Blane.

Mother's father, Henry Normal Powell was, according to the marriage certificate, "deceased," as was her mother.

However Great Grandmother Margaret E Millar was still alive and she lived in Aylesbury with Mother and Father. (The marriage certificate of Grandfather and Grandmother Powell shows her and her father's name as Miller, with an e.)

My parents moved to Railway Terrace, Bletchley, soon after they were married. Their son Charles was born in 1905, followed by Henry James (1907), Donald Fraser (1908) and Robert (1911).

In about 1913 the family, comprising Mother, Father, Great Grandmother Millar and four children, moved to 14 Brooklands Road. Sister Margaret (1914) was followed by Bernard (1915), Jack (1918) and Martin (1920).

Great Grandmother Margaret E Millar died in 1916 and was buried in Fenny Stratford cemetery.

Mother died 1st June 1971, was cremated at Milton near Northampton and her ashes deposited near those of her husband, Charles Henry.

Jack Blane
(*Undated*)

The Brooklands Road house had three bedrooms.

Parents slept in one bedroom, Margaret Millar in the second. The boys all had to share the third bedroom and its double bed, sometimes sleeping "top to tail."

After the death of Margaret Millar, their sister Margaret was moved out of her parents' room and had a bedroom to herself.

JEAN

LIFE IN POST-WAR BRITAIN

It was still a time of austerity, with rationing of nearly all goods and food not just continuing but extended. It was 1946 that actually saw the introduction of rationing for the basic foodstuffs such as bread and potatoes. Coal was also rationed, as were petrol, clothing and furniture. Clothing and furniture carried the 'Utility' trademark, a remnant of the war years.

As late as December 1947 a buying permit was still needed to buy furniture, and then priority was given to those such as servicemen returning and setting up homes, and newlyweds. The total allowance of coupons for furniture was 60 per household.

Certain conditions had to be met before anyone could apply to buy furniture. If any furniture was already in the house, or there was built-in furniture, then the allowance was reduced accordingly. The only available choices were from the illustrated copy of the Utility catalogue, used by all manufacturers.

To save fuel, the firm chosen to supply the furniture had to be based within 15 miles of the delivery address. In some cases it was necessary to obtain a buying permit and priority docket to purchase curtaining and floor covering. Finally, stocks were so low that immediate delivery was not always possible.

The typical cost of a dining room suite (table, chairs and sideboard), two easy chairs and a dressing table was £68 and 38 units of coupons. Little was left from the allowance of 60 coupons for other furniture: wardrobe 12 units, bed 5 units, kitchen cabinet 8 units and so on. Every piece of furniture had a points value. The Board of Trade Utility Furniture Office in Southport controlled all of this.

Many goods were only available with coupons - even sweets (candy, lollies), which like butter were rationed to 2 ounces per person per week until 1953. Some rationing extended further, into 1954. Cost was also a deterrent to buying anything unnecessary, when one considers that the average wage at this time was in the region of £6 per week. A police constable received a salary of £273 per year: £5/5/- (£5.25) per week.

For quite a number of years, running into the mid-late 1950s, purchase tax was imposed, similar to the present-day VAT, GST, or sales tax - but at the stratospheric rate of 33% on common everyday items. This rate was doubled to 66% for so-called luxuries such as refrigerators, wirelesses (radios) and jewellery.

Nothing was available to excess as it was either rationed or one could simply not afford it. Beer increased in price and a bottle of whisky now cost £1/11/- (£1.55), a good quarter of an average week's pay. A ladies' cardigan cost £4/3/- (£4.15) and six coupons. Both knitting and sewing were far more than just hobbies!

In today's money, nearly everything seems extremely cheap - but not by the wages of the time. As I say, in 1947 the average wage was just £6 per week. Even by 1961, when I had started working, £15/10/- (£15.50) per week was the average weekly wage for men (no thought of equal pay). It puts the relative costs in perspective.

Dad, returning to a fairly junior job in the wages section of the London Brick Company personnel department at Newton Longville near Bletchley after 6½ years in the army, earned less than the average wage in 1946.

By the time Dad left the Newton Longville works in 1954 he was earning £10/10/- per week. He was given a pay rise of 10 shillings, bringing him up to £11, to move to Stewartby as Social and Sports Club Secretary. The rent for our first house in Whiteley Crescent (including rates, now council or house tax) was £1 per week.

Our next house three years later, back in Bletchley, was older with just two bedrooms, and about the same rent. Because the house we then moved to in Stewartby was owned and subsidised by the brick company the rent there was still only just over £1 in 1954.

Most labourers, blue and white collar workers too, rented their homes. And very few people had cars. Dad could have learned to drive in the army, during the war. But cars cost around a year's wages at that time and Dad thought he would never be able to afford one. So he did not bother to learn to drive, either then or later, and in fact never did own a car.

No ordinary working people went abroad for holidays. There were far fewer planes, those there were being much smaller than now, and no low cost flights or package holidays. All air fares were, in comparative terms, far more expensive than today's.

There were no credit or debit cards and there was very little borrowing, although some goods could be bought on credit by Hire Purchase (HP) - or "tick" as it was known colloquially. But this was rather frowned on. People usually saved until they had the money to buy what they wanted.

Many people did not even have bank accounts. Their wages were paid in cash and they made all their payments the same way. The rent collector came around weekly for his money, as did the insurance man.

Perhaps I had better explain a bit about the pre-decimal currency. It was generally referred to as LSD: nothing to do with the drug that came later!

Strangely the L, written £, stood for pounds sterling, the S for shillings and the D for pence. Both the S and D were written in lower case when in actual use.

This currency is in what is called the duodecimal system, with 12 pence in a shilling. There were 20 shillings in a pound. It sounds complicated now but we didn't think anything of it, knowing nothing else.

All measures were imperial, including area and weight, which again would probably seem complicated to most of those growing up today, although we do still use some of the old ones

England, and certainly where we lived, was very mono-cultural. I don't remember knowing anyone who was not basically of white Anglo-Saxon origin, other than the Italian ice cream men who came round with their van in Beighton, until we moved to Stewartby and had a Yugoslavian neighbour.

There were so many things we did not have that are taken completely for granted now. Some had just not been invented and some were simply out of the reach of ordinary people.

There were no personal computers, cordless or mobile (cell) phones, game boys, personal music players, microwaves, dish washers etc. As for space travel: that really was the stuff of science fiction!

Cars did not have seat belts fitted as standard until 1987. There were no child and infant safety seats either. Babies might be placed in a carrycot on the back seat but an infant or young child would often be held in the arms, or sit on the knee, of a car passenger.

Pedal cyclists did not wear helmets and motorcycle helmets were not compulsory.

Of course, there were far fewer cars on the road than today.

Some acceptable fashion customs were quite different. For example, not many people other than gypsies even had pierced ears until about the time I started secondary education. And I don't remember any other kind of body piercing. Very few people other than sailors or fairground workers had tattoos and all of those so far as I knew were men.

Vegetarianism was looked upon by most people almost as if it were some strange cult. There were no specific vegetarian foods for sale in the shops or restaurants. The popular image was of rather peculiar, sandal wearing folk, eating nut cutlets (even though we had no real idea what a nut cutlet might be).

Having been born towards the end of World War II I spent my childhood living in the Cold War era. There was a continuing tense standoff between the Soviet Union, as it was then, and the West. Each side had nuclear weapons and the threat of nuclear war could feel very real.

On another sobering note, although we had no HIV or Aids, Swine or Bird Flu, MRSA or Covid-19, medicine was far from as advanced as now. There were fewer treatments or procedures and things were often much cruder. We did not have keyhole surgery and there was no chance of an organ transplant, for example, let alone gene therapy.

Many drugs that we have now were also unthought-of. There were fewer vaccines, which meant that even childhood illnesses could be much more serious.

I was almost ten years old before the first polio vaccine was developed. Even then it did not reach England for another couple of years. Polio was a devastating disease, especially for children, and an epidemic was very frightening. Thank goodness "Iron Lungs" and the devastating effects of polio are in the past for almost the whole world.

Although there were now vaccines for diseases such as diphtheria, children were still at risk of serious complications and even death from others like measles, mumps and whooping cough. Sadly, with some children not having the MMR vaccine, this is again becoming the case.

I did not know anyone who had a home phone until after we moved to Stewartby, and then only those in quite high positions in the brick company.

If you needed to make a telephone call you had to use a public phone box: for example, if you needed the doctor urgently. If you had a less urgent medical problem, you just went down to the surgery and it was first come, first seen.

I was six years old before I even saw a television set. Our family did not have one of our own until I was thirteen. The pictures were all in black and white, no colour sets, and in the early years the sets were mostly really bulky, with very small screens.

At first the UK had just one channel, the BBC. Then by the time we had our TV set, which stood on legs and had a rather smaller case and somewhat larger screen, we had the one BBC channel and the commercial channel ATV. That was it!

On a weekday the programmes started in the afternoon and ended at 11pm, when the channels stopped broadcasting. At the weekend I know there were some morning programmes too, by at least the time I was ten years old.

Televisions and wirelesses were both powered by valves, which could burn out and need replacing. These sets took quite a while to warm up too, when you switched them on, and of course no remote controls.

We had a large wireless with a dial that lit up and a number of knobs. I don't even know what all of them were for! There were two main stations, both BBC.

My Auntie Nellie and Uncle Reg in Bletchley had a wind-up gramophone (record player) that played 78rpm records. We had boxes of steel needles that needed very frequent changing. As the mechanism wound down, the record would get slower and the sound lower and more distorted. Wind it up again and the sound got higher and faster as you did so: great fun for children!

None of the houses I knew had central heating. There was an open coal fire in the living room (which went out at night) and sometimes in other rooms too, although those would seldom be lit. In the kitchen there was usually a boiler, which burned coke or anthracite (treated, harder and slower burning coal) that heated the water.

These boilers were rather like the large, round, black, wood burning stoves, with a solid door very low down for taking out the ashes and a lid on top, where the fuel was poured in from a hod.

The slow-burning fire in these would stay in overnight.

The coal men delivered the fuel and emptied it from their sacks into the coal barn.

The chimney sweep came in summer. That was a really messy job in those days. There was no vacuum sweeping. Everything possible would be moved out of the living room, and all that could not be moved covered in old sheets to keep off the soot, before the sweep started. He would push his sweep's brush, attached to the first pole, into the chimney. Then he would add one pole after another as he pushed upwards, until his brush came out at the top.

If we were at home when the sweep came, we children would go outside and let him know when we saw the brush poking out. He did have a sack at the bottom of the chimney to catch most of the soot. Dad kept that as fertilizer for the garden and allotment. Even so, when the sweep had gone there was a lot of cleaning up still to do. The freestanding boiler chimney did not get such a buildup of soot, as coke and anthracite burn more cleanly.

Some houses still had a range in the kitchen, a coal fire with an oven built in alongside it. You quite often see them depicted in old films. A kettle might sit on an iron trivet above the fire, which could also heat water in a boiler on the other side. The ranges were cleaned with lead blacking, which was rubbed in well with a cloth and then polished to a shine.

In the winter everywhere except our living room and kitchen would be really cold, almost like being in a garage or shed. Ice crystals formed patterns on the inside of the windows when it was very frosty. There were even times when, in the bedrooms, we could see our breath as we exhaled.

The houses were among the earliest in the UK to be built with cavity walls, although with no added insulation. High up, one inner brick might be left missing from an outer wall of a room. The outer brick here had a lot of little square holes through it for ventilation and was known as an airbrick.

That was fine in the summer but just added to the coldness in winter. So Dad would cut a piece of leftover linoleum (lino) to fit the gap and wedge it against the airbrick. This at least stopped the wind whistling into the room.

We had no fitted carpets, just lino on the floor, with rugs. There was a rug next to the bed and if your feet missed it on a winter morning, you knew it! Instead of duvets (unheard of, at least in our family) we had sheets and blankets, with an eiderdown (thick quilt) on top.

Every night in winter we all had hot water bottles in our beds. The sheets were so cold until your feet got down to that. It was wonderful to feel its heat.

In the summer our living room fire would not be lit at all and our boiler only once a week, for baths and for washing clothes. The rest of the time water was boiled in a kettle on the stove for us to have a good wash over. The bathroom was heated by an Aladdin brand paraffin stove in winter.

Later, when I was about thirteen years old, we had an electric wall heater in the bathroom. We also had an electric immersion heater fitted in the hot water tank. Now we could have hot water all through the year, without the boiler *or* a kettle!

The first shower I saw was in 1955, when I was ten years old. There were two cold-water showers in each set of changing rooms at Stewartby swimming pool, for rinsing off the chlorine.

There were no automatic washing machines and no dryers. The whites (all cotton in the post-war years) would be boiled in a special washing boiler, which by now was at least electric. To make the white clothes brighter, Mum also added what was called a blue bag to their wash water.

When I was very young all the clothes were rubbed on a scrubbing board with bar soap to get them clean. The clothes and linen were taken out of the hot water with long, wooden handled wash tongs, and left until cool enough to handle.

After washing, and again after rinsing, everything was put through the two wooden rollers of the mangle, turned by hand, to wring them out. The boiler, put on first thing in the morning, filled the kitchen with steam.

Later Mum had an electric washing machine: a tub with a paddle to agitate the clothes and an electric mangle integral to it. But there was no automatic fill or empty, and no spin action.

When spin dryers came along, they took out more water than the mangle but you had to keep an eye on the outlet pipe in the sink!

Doing the washing, pegging it out and clearing away took up the whole of Monday morning. Then all the washing had to be taken in from the line later and folded. There were very few synthetics and no easy-care fabrics, so nearly everything needed ironing too.

If the weather was too bad to get the clothes dry outside, they were hung on a line across the kitchen, keeping it steamed up for hours.

Ironing was a job for Monday evening or Tuesday. Mum did have an electric iron but it had no thermostat and no steam, so ironing was quite a skilled job.

With all this, it is little wonder that we did not change our clothes too frequently. Bedding was changed once a week but only the bottom sheet from each bed was washed. The top sheet became the bottom sheet, with a clean one over it. This was known as "topping and tailing."

All male office workers wore white shirts and a tie, hence the term White Collar Workers. These white cotton shirts lasted longer, and were freshened up between washes, by having detachable collars. The collars and necks of the shirts had very small buttonholes in them.

Little double headed collar buttons (collar studs) passed through these holes to keep the collar in place. This meant that the collar alone could be changed daily, rather than the whole shirt.

Those who could afford it might send washing to the laundry. It would be collected at the door and delivered back wrapped in brown paper tied with string.

I only knew about this because although my Auntie Nellie washed most of their clothes herself, she did send the sheets and my Uncle Reg's butcher's overalls and aprons, to the Co-op (Co-operative Society) laundry once a week.

All housework took a lot of doing. In my earlier years every floor and any big rug had to be swept with a brush. Tile and lino floors were also scrubbed with a scrubbing brush. That was a hands and knees job. The small rugs were taken out and shaken every week.

Larger rugs were taken out less frequently, hung over the clothesline and beaten with a carpet beater to get out all the dust and grime.

The carpet beaters we had were woven cane, shaped rather like a Celtic knot on the end of a handle, as you see in the picture.

Mum also had a manual carpet sweeper of the kind you can still buy today.

In the winter the living room needed a thorough clean every day. Ash and coal dust would have settled everywhere, however careful you were.

The grate was emptied of ash first thing in the morning, after it had cooled down overnight. Crumpled newspaper was placed on the grate, sticks layered on it, with a few pieces of coal placed on top of them.

The paper was lit in several places, hopefully the fire caught, and then more coal would be tipped on. If the wind was in the wrong direction and the fire wouldn't catch, you'd hold a sheet of newspaper across it to funnel air through the kindling up into the chimney.

But be careful! If the draught dragged in the paper and it caught fire you had to let go of it pretty smartly.

Every house had a front doorstep and most a back one too, which would be scrubbed every week. This was usually on the same day as the drains were cleaned, the grates over the drains being thoroughly scoured as well.

We had metal dustbins and there were no bin liners. So the dustbin too needed a regular scouring. Even the draining boards by the sink were given a good scrub every week, being wooden.

While she was working Mum always had the wireless on, mainly music. Her favourite singer was Bing Crosby. I remember Housewives' Choice at 9.00am every weekday, with Workers' Playtime later in the morning. The latter came live from a work's canteen somewhere, supposedly in the mid-morning tea break, and was comedy and music.

Sunday lunchtimes there was a programme of requests called Family Favourites. On a Saturday morning we listened to Children's Choice, a programme of musical requests made by - you've got it - children. A number and variety of comedy programmes were also very popular.

Dad always worked within cycling distance of home. Every day he came back for his midday meal, which was our dinner. Carole and I of course came home for dinner too, until we went on the bus to Bedford to school.

All tea had to be made in the pot with loose leaves. After leaving it to brew, the tea was poured through a strainer laid across the top of the cup. This caught most of the leaves. But if you drank to the bottom of the cup, you still got a mouthful of the smallest ones. Ugh! That made you careful.

There were no tea bags or instant tea and both were also pretty nasty when they did first go on sale.

There wasn't much choice of breakfast cereal: none of the sugared, flavoured ones until Frosties and Sugar Puffs came along.

All I recall being available in the cereal line were cornflakes, puffed wheat, shredded wheat and Weetabix, with porridge in the winter. Honor has reminded me that the Co-op also sold Grape Nuts!

When we weren't at school we usually had a cup of milky Camp coffee with chicory essence, and a biscuit, for "elevenses" in the morning with Mum. Coffee had been very scarce in the war and chicory used as a substitute.

Camp, in its distinctive bottle, has a sweetish flavour all its own and indescribable. Some people love it and it's still on sale now, although the label design has been slightly changed to show the two characters as equals.

I don't know whether it was partly because sugar was rationed until I was eight years old, and we craved sweetness, but we all took two teaspoonfuls of sugar in our tea and coffee.

On the other hand, nearly everyone did take sugar in those days. Uncle Reg had three heaped teaspoons of sugar in his hot drinks. We always drank our tea and coffee from a cup and saucer, never a mug

Included in our weekly sugar ration was 2oz of sweets per person. Mum always bought four separate paper bags of different loose sweets, which were kept in an old metal lunch tin. There weren't any left at the end of each week. I think I have probably never consistently eaten sweets in that way since.

For dinner we always had a main course and a dessert, known as pudding or afters. I don't know why "pudding" because the steamed desserts were specifically known as pudding, as were milk puddings such as rice pudding and sago. We called the latter frog's eggs because it was just like a cloud of frogspawn in the milk, only without the black eye in each egg.

Our usual main course would be meat, with potatoes and a seasonal vegetable. Mum always poured homemade gravy on our dinner unless we had a beef stew or a casserole, which came with their own.

Once a week on a Friday Mum made fresh fried fish and chips (no gravy on that either!). I am sure that Uncle Reg being a butcher helped with us always having good quality meat to eat.

I knew nothing at all of "foreign" foods until I was well into my teens. The only pasta I ate as a child was macaroni, cooked as a milk pudding and known by us as pipe pudding. I didn't even have macaroni cheese until I had school dinners at Bedford High School

We ate nothing grilled that I recall, other than toast, and in winter we often cooked that and crumpets on a toasting fork over the living room fire. We did not have a toaster, just the grill on the cooker.

Meat was roasted, stewed, braised or fried. The frying was done in beef lard. I don't think we had any choice of cooking oils in the post-war years, anyway.

Olive oil was used - but not for cooking. Highly processed, very far from virgin, olive oil was bought in small bottles from the chemist (pharmacy). It was used to treat earache.

A few drops would be warmed and drizzled into the affected ear. It was quite soothing but I don't know if it did any good beyond that.

Healthy eating was never an issue. We simply ate what there was. In any case, nearly all our food was fresh and we had little in the way of snacks. We did eat more fried and fatty food than is now considered good for you but also a lot of fresh vegetables, with no real junk food.

We used up more energy too, not least keeping up our body temperature in the winter cold, but also in walking or cycling nearly everywhere and, for us children, playing outside. Even those who owned cars didn't use them for short distances.

Mum wore her old clothes and old laddered stockings (a ladder is a run) in the mornings to do her housework.

Following dinner, she always washed herself well at the kitchen sink after we'd had a cup of tea and she had washed the dishes. After her wash Mum changed into good clothes and stockings even if she was not going out.

We had a cup of tea with Mum in the middle of the afternoon that was timed, once we had started school, for just after we arrived home.

Mum generally did some knitting in the afternoon, and she'd maybe read her Woman's Weekly magazine. She also got knitting patterns, which it still carries, from the magazine. You can see some of those in the next picture.

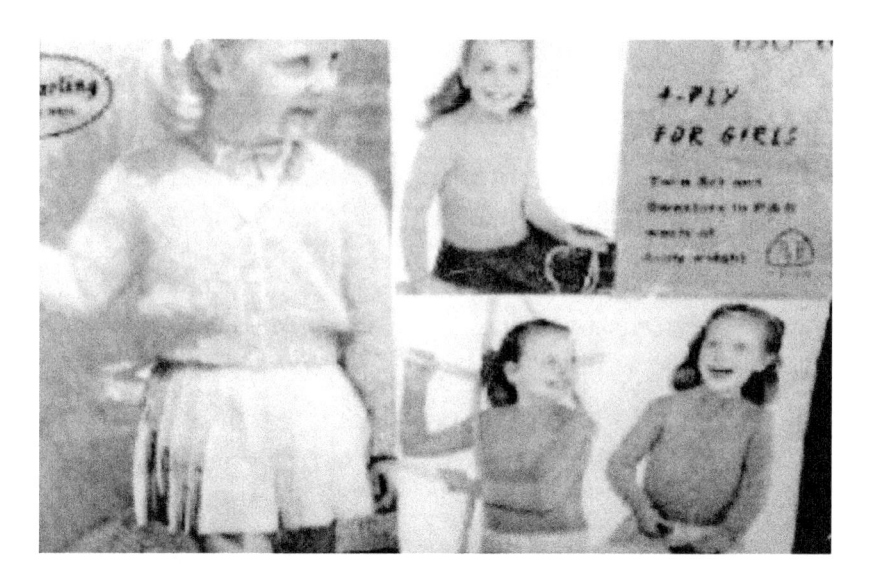

All the magazines were made from very thin paper (like newspaper) for some years after the war. There were no colour pictures in them either.

Mum knitted all the family warm sweaters and cardigans during these years. The wool came in skeins, long loops twisted round in sort of figures of eight, as in the picture.

To use it, you first untwisted the skein. Then it had to be rewound. I quite often sat with my forearms straight out in front of me, the skein looped over them and pulled tight.

Mum took an end and away she went, winding it from the skein into a ball. But holding the skein for long made my arms ache and begin to droop.

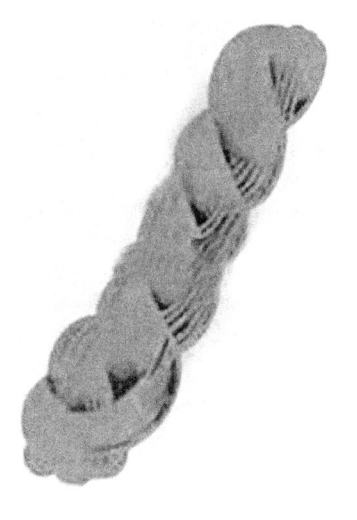

When we were very young, Mum made our dresses from simple patterns on an old hand worked Singer sewing machine, just like the one shown here.

In the early days Mum made all her own curtains too. Although still rationed after the war, you could get more fabric for your coupons than you could pairs of ready-made curtains, even if you could find those to buy.

Everyone also darned socks. The area with the hole was stretched over a wooden "mushroom" and wool of an appropriate colour was woven back and forth across the hole with a large darning needle.

Men's jackets had the elbows patched with pieces of leather when they became very worn, to make them last longer too. Make do and mend was the watchword.

Our old cotton sheets were also mended on the Singer machine. As the middle wore out before the sides, a sheet would be cut right down the centre and the two outer edges sewn together, to become the new middle. (Got that?) What had now become the worn outer edges were then hemmed. This was known as "sides to middling." That was real make do and mend!

Like most mothers then, Mum did not work outside the home. The husband went out to work to earn the money to keep his family.

The wife did all the work in the home and cared for the children. This was generally felt to be a fair division of labour in many households.

And it was nearly all "husband and wife." Hardly any unmarried couples lived together, generally thought of as living in sin. There were also few single parent families, other than where a parent had been widowed.

For one thing, for a woman to have a child out of wedlock was a real disgrace. For another, divorce was very difficult and expensive. There were not the same kinds of benefits available then as now either.

Mum, like many other women, preserved fruit for eating in winter, and with fruit and vegetables made jams and chutneys. The latter were rather along the lines of Branston type pickle or relishes.

She also pickled onions and red cabbage. The fruit, onions and red cabbage were kept in big jars (Kilner jars): the fruit in syrup, the onions and red cabbage in seasoned vinegar.

One reason for preserving in this way was that home refrigerators and freezers were very uncommon. The first I owned of either was in Montana in 1965.

But now things have come full circle. More people are again making preserves of various kinds.

What houses did have then was a walk-in larder or pantry. This usually led off from the kitchen, in the coolest part of the house. In ordinary houses it was a very small room with shelves for storing bottles, jars, tins (cans) and packets.

Along one wall was a shelf, a thick marble or concrete slab. It was for putting things on that needed keeping cold: the likes of butter, milk and cheese. Beneath it was a meat safe, a cupboard with a wire mesh door, both for keeping the meat cool and keeping flies out.

In really hot weather the milk stood in a bucket of cold water to stop it souring. Although by the mid 1950s some frozen foods were available, such as fish fingers, they had to be eaten within a day or so as they could not be kept longer without a freezer.

The only real convenience foods then that I remember, in addition to tinned foods, were gravy powder (Bisto) and stock cubes (Oxo), Bird's custard, blancmange powders, jelly (Jell-O) cubes, biscuits (cookies) and crackers.

Mum always made her own mint sauce and applesauce. We might occasionally have a shop bought cake but mostly Mum made these too. The only fast-food outlets and takeaways were fish and chip shops. The choice there was either fish or fish cakes.

There were no convenience pet foods either. Once a week Uncle Reg drove to Bedford to buy cheap meat especially for use as pet food. We reckoned it was horsemeat or the some such.

He did have big walk-in refrigerators at the back of the butcher's shop he managed in Bletchley so all the meat kept fresh, although there were no refrigerated display areas. The meat was cut to order on wooden topped counters, kept well scrubbed.

In the earlier years of my life nearly all types of dry foods were sold loose by weight. And throughout my childhood milk was delivered to the doorstep in pint bottles daily from Monday to Saturday. It was full cream milk, as there was no semi-skimmed or skimmed (that I ever saw).

The milk was not homogenised as now but had a layer of cream on top. Mostly, the bottle would be shaken to mix the milk and cream. On a Sunday though we sometimes had "top of the milk" on tinned fruit for tea.

You could also buy sterilised milk. This came in a bottle similar in shape to a wine bottle, with a cap like that on a beer bottle. So it was easy to tell which was which.

This sterilised milk was rather like tinned evaporated milk. It was nice in coffee and for baking but I thought that it made tea taste really peculiar.

The baker's van came round daily too in the week, with freshly baked uncut loaves and rolls. We didn't have sliced, packaged bread.

At Bletchley, the milk came from the Co-op dairy and the bread from their bakery. Mum bought milk and bread checks at the Co-op shop. These were plastic tokens.

She would leave milk tokens out with the empty bottles on the doorstep, for however many pints she wanted. The man who delivered the bread was paid with the bread tokens. If you weren't in, you could leave a bag containing your bread token hanging on the front door knob.

As I say, we had no sliced bread and the bread varieties were just white and wholemeal, the latter much less common than now, although we could buy different shaped loaves. We always had white bread for cutting, usually a farmhouse loaf.

I liked the crusty cottage loaf Mum sometimes bought. This is one smaller round of dough on top of a large one. Even better were the little cottage loaf shaped rolls. Miniature wholemeal Hovis loaves were a treat too, split and buttered.

Meat and fish were bought fresh, as they would not keep for long without refrigeration. There was at least one fishmonger in every town, as well as a butcher.

In the villages a van selling wet (fresh, raw) fish often came around once a week on a Friday. The fish was mainly cod and both fresh and smoked haddock.

Vegetables and fruit were mostly seasonal, other than tinned of course. It was too expensive to fly in goods for the general market. Citrus fruits from the Mediterranean came in by boat, as did bananas from the Caribbean.

We could buy grapes and sometimes saw fresh pineapples, peaches and apricots. They were all quite expensive though. I really don't remember any fresh vegetables being brought in.

There were no sell by, best before, or use by dates on foods. Common sense, sight and smell had to be your guide!

For her main groceries Mum had an order book with carbon paper, with each order page having its copy. After making her list, she took the book to the Co-op.

She left it there and her order was made up, with the prices written next to each item and totalled. The shop kept the top copy and the order was then delivered on a set day each week with the returned order book. Mum could see how much she owed and pay the bill. This was again normal practice.

Speaking of paying bills reminds me of something else. Being paid in cash like most workers, Dad kept a small portion of his weekly pay for spending money. Mum had an old cash tin in which she put the rest. It was divided between the various compartments, so much for rent, for groceries, the electric bill and so on.

Whenever you bought anything at the Co-op, which owned all kinds of shops and even department stores, you got a receipt that was like a little ticket. The total you had spent and your dividend number were hand-written on this. These tickets were in sheets, again in a carboned book so that the Co-op had a copy too.

As the customers of the Co-op were its shareholders, every customer had a dividend number and each year the net profit was divided up between them. You received a dividend payment proportional to what you had spent.

There were no supermarkets. The very first self-service shop in England, Sainsbury's (now a supermarket chain), opened in London in 1950 but these did not start to reach us for a few more years.

In ordinary shops there might be some items on display that you could pick up and take to the counter but generally you asked for what you wanted and the shop assistant got it for you.

Shops closed for one afternoon each week, the same day for all the shops in each town, usually a Wednesday or Thursday. This was known as early closing, or half-day closing, day. With the staff working Saturdays, it gave them an extra half-day off.

Nearly all shops closed on Sunday, although newsagents delivered the newspapers as they did every other day (magazines and comics were also delivered), and opened for a few hours. It was the same with Bank Holidays and I don't remember any shop that was open on Good Friday, Easter Sunday, Christmas Day or Boxing Day.

One quirky thing was that on a Sunday, although shops could sell food that was ready to eat, no shop was allowed to sell food that needed cooking.

The only shop I remember being open on a Sunday when we lived in Bletchley was Golding's, where you could buy homemade vanilla ice cream. You could buy cones or take your own bowl there to be filled. That ice cream was *really* creamy and delicious.

There was a very good postal (mail) service. Letters were all one price to send, no two-tier system, and nearly always arrived by the next day. There were two deliveries a day, one early in the morning (often before breakfast) and then another in the afternoon. What we didn't have was all the junk mail.

Crime rates were quite low. Gun crime in England was extremely rare then. I am afraid we associated that kind of crime with America. I don't remember ever hearing anything about an illegal drug trade either, though I am sure some went on. But again, it wasn't that prevalent.

On the other side of the coin, suicide and abortion were both crimes - and crimes such as domestic violence and abuse tended to often go unreported and unpunished, even more so than now.

It's odd sometimes, the things you remember. I hated the toilet paper we had to use. It was in sheets, pulled out of a box rather than on a roll, although the box fitted into a wall holder. And it was so hard and stiff. The closest thing I can describe it to is being nearly like greaseproof paper (not quite as thick and shiny as waxed paper).

You pulled out a sheet, about the same size as a sheet of soft toilet roll, crumpled it and rubbed it between your hands to soften it. How it ever absorbed anything, I do not know.

At Stewartby Dad still used the old hard stuff for several years after the rest of us had taken to the now available soft toilet paper. That meant we had to keep two lots of paper on the toilet wall.

Throughout the post-war years we had no other kind of disposable wipes. For example, we had no paper tissues but used our cotton handkerchiefs, which Mum boil washed.

Spills and mess were all cleaned up with cloths, which would be not just washed but boil washed, regularly. The aforementioned greaseproof paper was the only wrap we had, no foil and no clingfilm.

There were also no plastic bags, including carrier bags. You just took your own shopping bags or baskets with you. That is again something coming full circle.

We didn't have plastic bottles and I don't remember drinks in cans, either. You paid a deposit when you bought drinks in glass bottles. This was returned when you took the bottles back. We children would sometimes take back bottles in return for keeping the few pence deposit.

There was still a comprehensive rail network crisscrossing the whole country, reaching most towns and villages. The line from Bletchley to Bedford was a section of the longer Oxford to Cambridge line. The rest of that line and many others were axed in the 1960s, when the network was greatly reduced.

On the remaining section of our local line, along with the normal railway stations were several "Halts." Their platforms were like very low decking, more or less at road level.

Using their steam, the trains let down a set of steps from the guard's van at the halts, for passengers' use. Large items such as prams and bicycles were manhandled on to the train.

When diesel took over from steam power, raised platforms were built and the halts were no more.

I could go on reminiscing but it's all in my childhood memoir, "Bucks, Beds and Bricks," the first book I wrote.

My memories here are those that I thought the most relevant to my father's story.

BACK TO JACK'S LIFE

The earliest story I have of Dad is as a two-year old, when Martin was born - at home, like all the children. Taken into the bedroom to see the new baby, Dad just climbed onto the bed to snuggle up to his mother.

Martin was weak in his early years, and his parents were told not to let him weight bear. His legs were splinted and for 3-4 years he was taken out by his brothers in a pushchair. Sometimes the brothers would argue whose turn it was to push "Little Mate," leaving him to wait patiently until they collected him once more.

One day a group of the brothers set off downhill to the brook at the end of the road. Martin's pushchair got away from them and ended up in the brook. The other boys jumped in to get him and the pushchair out, soaking themselves.

You can imagine the trouble they were in when they arrived home. The house had no washing machine, and no dryer of course. The boys didn't have many spare clothes, let alone boots. Shall we just say that their mother was not amused!

Something Dad enjoyed as a treat was travelling on the train from Bletchley to Cow Bridge Halt, the last stop before Bedford, to visit an aunt and uncle who lived close by in Elstow village.

From his teens Dad cycled almost everywhere, right up until his eyesight made it too dangerous for him. In his youth he belonged to a cycling club. He and Martin took part in races and also long-distance trips, cycling into Wales and back in a day on one occasion. Dad said they always took dates with them to eat, to keep them going.

Quite often on a Sunday afternoon in the summer, when Carole was old enough, we went for a family bike ride from Stewartby. It certainly wasn't anything like the rides Dad did as a young man. But we went to Ampthill Park (pushing our bikes up the steep hill) or around local villages. I think we all enjoyed those. And rather than taking dates to eat, Dad might buy us an ice cream!

We also still went primrosing in the Spring, packing bunches in moss to send up to Aunt Annie in Beighton. But now primroses are a protected species.

When we lived in Bletchley and Far Bletchley, Dad cycled to work every Monday to Friday. He came home for dinner before going back to work for the afternoon. Then once he'd cycled home after work at 5 o'clock, he had finished for the day.

It was very different at Stewartby, running the Club. Dad's basic days were the same but it was a good thing he lived much closer to his workplace.

At Stewartby, Dad's work did not always end when he came home at 5 o'clock for his tea. Because he ran the club Dad was also down there on Monday evenings for the Tote, a kind of raffle where people had the same numbers every week.

Then he was there at Sunday dinnertime for ordinary raffles as well, before coming home to eat. We would occasionally hear loud knocking on the front door at night too. If the village bobby found the club unsecured or the burglar alarm went off, Dad as keyholder would be called out.

It didn't take long for the young lads of the village to get to know Dad. If any of them were hanging around the club, or underage youths trying to get in, he was soon there sorting them out. They grumbled about him but respected him.

When adult they all liked him and enjoyed remembering, and telling the stories of, his strictness because he was also always (or nearly always!) fair.

Our first autumn in Stewartby we discovered that we were to see very little of Dad each year in the few months before Christmas.

With so much extra work to do, he went back to the club after tea on most evenings.

What took up Dad's time in the run up to Christmas? First of all, there were Christmas parties for the primary school age children. The brick company paid for everything but Dad did all of the organising.

These parties were not just for the children of Stewartby workers but also for those in little brickworks either side of Stewartby and a number of other small brickworks around Peterborough.

With so many children to cater for, parties were held over several Saturday afternoons before Christmas. They all took place in Stewartby village hall, with transport laid on for those who had to travel.

Dad had to work out numbers and arrange for everything, including not only the catering, the entertainer, and the transport, but the volunteers too, who helped at each of the parties.

He also had to buy a present for each and every child. As you see here, Father Christmas came in his traditional red, fur trimmed hooded robe, to hand them out at all the parties.

Presents were bought by age and sex, so for example every five-year-old girl had the same present and so on. These presents were all wrapped, in a different paper for each age and sex. The children were even called by name to collect their presents. Dad and a colleague went to a toy wholesaler in Banbury in late summer every year to place the toy order.

Dad ordered the Christmas trees for the club and the village hall, ordering ours (and paying for it) at the same time.

Something I only found out years later is that, despite my parents having very little money, Dad bought a Christmas tree for an orphanage in Kempston every year until the orphanage closed - long after I had grown up.

New Year entertainment coach trips were organised for the older children. Dad booked seats for a pantomime or ice show in some large town, and again arranged the transport. Each child on these trips had a packed lunch type meal in a folded cardboard box.

Volunteer parents made the sandwiches and packed the meals at long tables in the club. Other parents accompanied the children on the coaches.

I went to parties and to the pantomimes and ice shows. We sat at long tables in the hall for the parties and I had never seen so many children in one room.

I remember a magician coming to entertain us one year and the parties were always good fun. So later were the coach trips themselves, as well as the shows we went to see. We usually had a sing-song on the way home.

The company's pensioners and widows were not forgotten either. Again, it was Dad who did all the practical work. Each of their households received a supply of coal and a chicken.

As Dad said, the men also had a bottle of whisky and the women a box of chocolates. I suppose that was sexism and as such might not seem acceptable nowadays, but I must say that nobody complained then. That's how things were and everyone seemed happy enough.

At the club there were whist drives and raffles for Christmas, with all kinds of festive prizes. Again, Dad did the buying. One raffle, known as the Fur and Feather although it was then only poultry, was for fresh turkeys and chickens that were to be delivered just before Christmas. There weren't any frozen birds.

Uncle Reg supplied the poultry at a good price. One year following that raffle, Dad was really teased at the club. He and Uncle had the first two winning raffle tickets. I think there were cries of foul - or was it *fowl*?

Dad was present at all the events, ensuring the smooth running of them. He delivered the gifts to the pensioners and widows too, except for the coal! He was generally offered a drink at various houses on his rounds.

One man made his own wine. It was, "Try this one" and, "This one's good this year." Dad soon learned to be wary, as these seemingly innocuous wines were really potent.

There were additional benefits, too. Travelling reps came to the club from the various suppliers to take orders for the beer, spirits, soft drinks and snacks the club sold.

At Christmas most of them gave presents to Dad. He always had malt whisky and vintage port, big boxes of chocolates, perhaps cigars. One year I remember he was given a box of twelve really deluxe Christmas crackers, and once just one huge cracker containing quite a number of lovely gifts.

Like most working men, Dad had a vegetable allotment. This was a standard plot size of 10 pole, used here as a measure of area. For allotments this usually translated to an actual size of 5½ x 55 yards.

Dad enjoyed his allotment, which was just as well since it was hard graft. It also gave us much needed fresh provisions.

Dad grew almost all of our vegetables, including potatoes. Some relatives and friends had fruit trees. They would pass on excess produce, Dad doing the same with his. He only gave up working an allotment after slipping a disc in his back.

It was while Dad was off work with his slipped disc that he taught me to play cribbage. He was a keen player himself and his teaching stood me in good stead in later years, especially last year when we were in Covid-19 lockdown. John and I had the cribbage board out several afternoons a week.

It's odd the things that come to mind. I had almost forgotten that Dad polished the shoes of the whole family for as long as I lived at home. He also helped Mum clean the oven thoroughly every Sunday, after the dinner dishes had been washed.

Dad and Uncle Reg, as you see them in the picture, were keen anglers. They went out most Sundays in the season while we lived at Bletchley, Dad often wearing this old leather army jerkin.

Dad (of course) usually cycled, carrying his fishing basket and rod over his shoulder. The River Ouzel and Grand Union Canal were popular fishing spots for both casual and competition angling.

Dad continued to enjoy his fishing after moving to Stewartby, even taking Carole and me with him on some occasions, as you see us here at Millbrook Pit (flooded knothole).

A keen competition angler, Dad won a number of trophies over the years

The competitions were often held some distance away, when the Angling Club members would take a company bus to the location.

The next picture shows Dad, on the left, ready for one such trip.

The big annual trophies had to be returned after a year but the commemorative spoons given with them were kept. I particularly remember one lovely big trophy.

The spoons were kept in our china cabinet but sadly, although I now have the china cabinet, I don't know what happened to those spoons.

Stephen Weeks, who lived in Stewartby as a boy, in Wavell Close, passed on this memory. He was given his first fishing rod by Dad, one made of split cane. He spent many happy hours fishing with it and remembers Dad as a very generous man.

LATER YEARS

For my father, family was what mattered most in life. Hence came his exhortation to us, "Keep family." He loved and cherished each of his grandchildren and great grandchildren as they came along. All were very special to him.

But this exhortation also covered extended family. Don's son Rex among others, though living in Canada, always kept in touch with Dad. I still keep contact with Rex and some other cousins, along with my more immediate family.

Another saying of Dad's concerned his will. With a good pension and no rent to pay, my parents were better off financially in retirement than they had ever been. Whilst not rich, they could afford to live comfortably and buy the things they wanted.

Dad used to say that his will would read, "Being of sound mind, I spent it!" Carole and I encouraged the sentiment. It's now passed into family lore, with us saying the same thing to our own children, who respond as we did.

Dad kept up with some of his army friends for many years. I think he felt it quite keenly when the last of them died in the 1990s. There was now nobody left who shared those wartime memories of his.

For some years after retiring, he and Mum attended reunions of his army unit, staying at Llandudno on the Welsh coast. Numbers here though, sadly dwindled also with each year that went by.

In his later years my father developed wet AMD (age-related macular degeneration), and his eyesight began to worsen. This was before the injections now available to really slow the rate of deterioration. Laser treatment was already in use and he did have that a few times but he eventually lost his central vision.

After his retirement Dad made handsewn soft toys that he either gave to charities to raffle, or sold and donated the proceeds. It was a sad day for him when he could no longer see well enough to sew. He'd given a toy to each of his great grandchildren. Mum loved them and had one of each

Poor Mum's arthritis had really degenerated and she had become very limited in what she was able to do, though still mobile and active. Her hands, neck and back were worst affected. It was a sad day for her too, when she had to finally give up her knitting.

Dad took over the housework at Wavell Close, almost it would seem coming full circle from his childhood. But, approaching 80, he told Mum that he too could no longer manage it. That's when he applied for a Sir Malcolm Stewart Trust home.

They lived in the bungalow for 12 years.

A bachelor friend, Mervyn (Merv) Bunker also lived in a bungalow. As he was on his own Mum and Dad would have him over to share Christmas Day with them, for as long as Mum could still cope.

Finding a lump in his neck in his mid-eighties, Dad went to the doctor. It transpired that this was a secondary from undiagnosed prostate cancer.

Dad was horrified. He'd had a prostatectomy years before, asked the surgeon to remove his prostate completely, and been assured that this was done.

The cancer had now spread throughout Dad's body, including his bones. It was too advanced for anything other than hormone treatment, which he was prescribed.

We were told that this might give him around two years symptom free. In fact it gave him a good few more. It seemed that when Dad died at 94 years old the symptoms were just beginning to return.

For some years after moving into the bungalow my parents still took the bus to Bedford once a week to have a pub lunch and perhaps do a bit of shopping.

One day Dad was standing at the roadside waiting for Mum, whom he'd left at a shop. He was carrying his white stick and some kind woman helped him across the road - from whence he had just come. Being the kind of man he was, Dad simply thanked her and waited to cross the road back.

Dad cycled from home to Stewartby Club for his two lunchtime pints and a chat with friends until well into his eighties.

Steve and Jude Hale, who ran Stewartby Club from 1996-2005, remember him as a member of the "Morning Club," which came in at the opening time of 11.00am.

Steve's nickname for the group was "The Stewartby Taliban,"

which he qualified by saying they were a nice version and a great "crack." But Dad was always a stickler for things being done right. Woe betide Steve if he opened a bit early!

Dad gave up cycling when his sight became too poor and his strength began to wane. Then his friend John Burston kindly picked him up by car, until the day came that Dad felt he could no longer leave Mum alone, with her now suffering from worsening dementia.

Dad was registered legally blind. He was supported by visits from a member of Blind Veterans UK. Sight Concern Bedford provided both support and aids to help with everyday living.

Even with Carole's help, a weekly cleaner and carers twice a day (hated by Mum) the time came in 2010 when Dad felt he couldn't cope anymore, especially as Mum's mental health deteriorated.

He was by then almost blind, physically weaker - and Mum was becoming ever more confused and distressed. My gentle mother could now be quite verbally aggressive towards Dad.

I think the final straw came when Mum was being particularly stubborn and aggressive. Poor Dad in frustration put his fist into the microwave. He was quite horrified at what he had done and afraid that one day he might strike out at Mum herself.

Despite this, to the end of his life Dad would say that how she had become wasn't Mum but the illness. To him she remained always his "darling."

We found a good care home, Salvete in Bedford, close to where Carole lives. The two of them moved in together just before their 70th Wedding Anniversary in October 2010. That anniversary was our last family celebration.

While Dad was happy and relieved at the move, Mum felt very differently. She would never have agreed to it if Dad hadn't been insistent, and she was never really happy there.

Dad was largely quite content and appreciated the care. But the one thing that upset him was when a German couple moved in.

He hated it when the man sat next to him, or on one occasion even sat in Dad's own recliner chair. The woman was pleasant but her husband could be quite rude.

Dad made his feelings known. Although those feelings may have been irrational, I think they were understandable in an old man who still had nightmares from his WWII experiences.

For two years Dad's physical health slowly deteriorated, as did Mum's mental health. Dad's memory became less certain as he aged, which he found frustrating at times, but he did not suffer from any form of dementia.

Dad eventually took to his bed, too weary to do anything else. But he remained content and always happy to see any of his family when we visited.

The following is the last picture I have of them together, after Dad had taken to his bed.

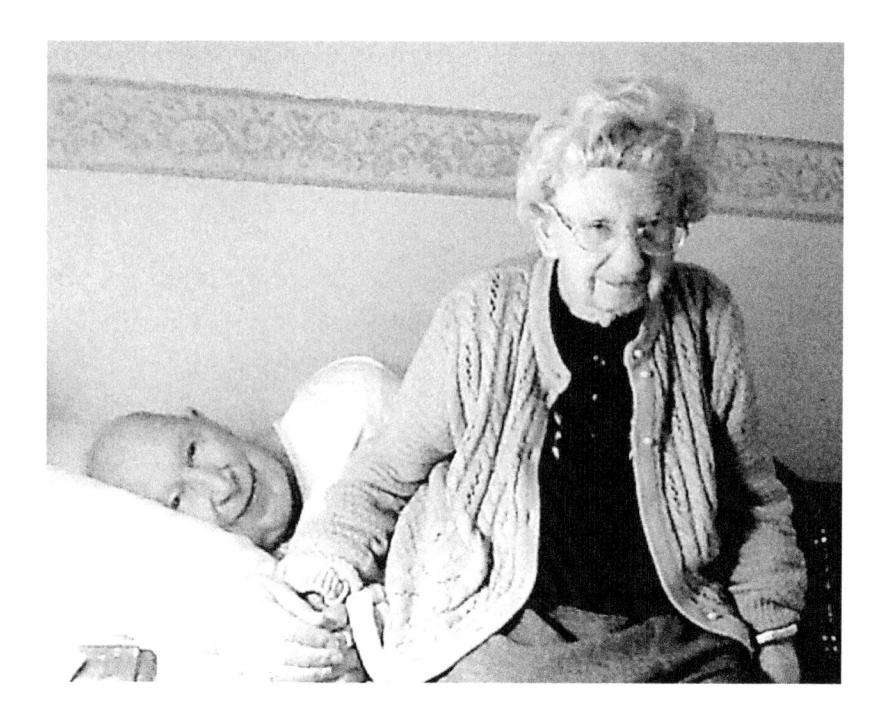

Carole and I were both with Dad when he died peacefully on the morning of 8 December 2012, at the age of 94. His funeral was held 21 December.

The following January Carole and I took Dad's ashes down to the river in Bedford, where it split in two for a distance.

We went to a fishing stage on what we called the back river and slowly, lovingly, tipped Dad's ashes into the water. They gurgled gently as they floated down into and along the current.

Dad hadn't wanted his ashes interred, he had loved his fishing, and this seemed appropriate.

So it was that on a cold, crisp winter morning, Carole and I said our final goodbyes.

Along the riverbank

Here is where Carole and I said our last goodbyes, as Dad slipped quietly into the water from this fishing stage.

My parents had always been a solid background to my life, their love and support unquestioned and completely unconditional.

I can't say that I really noticed them ageing until they were quite elderly. They were just Mum and Dad. But in their latter years it was hard to see them change so much, helpless to prevent it.

Jack's Darling, our lovely Mum Kitty, lived with her dementia for almost two years following his death.

She died in her sleep, also aged 94, the evening of 6 September 2014.

A TREASURED FAMILY LEGACY

For many years after WWII my father seemingly had no regard for these reminders of that conflict, although much later he did evidence a pride in them. All his grandchildren had an interest in his war history, Winn's being the strongest.

In his late eighties, Dad said that he wanted Winn to have his medals and medallion. Winn didn't want to take anything while my father was alive. I told him that knowing things were in safe keeping within the family would give his Grandad peace of mind.

So with a real sense of honour and privilege, Winn accepted gratefully. He had the medals and some photographs mounted behind museum quality glass, other memorabilia also mounted.

Winn in his turn has passed on these precious mementos to Luke, Dad's eldest great grandson, to ensure they remain in the family.

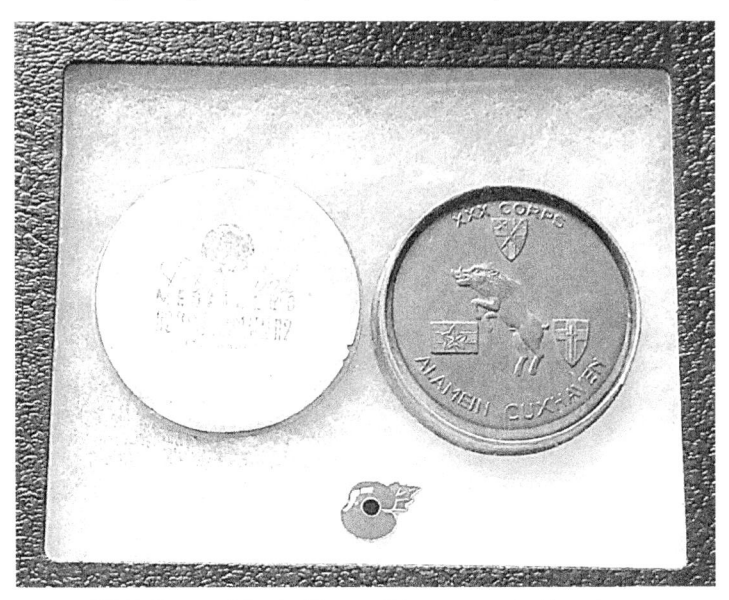

XXX Corps Medallion with presentation box
Poppy for remembrance

Jean Blane Flannery

IN MEMORIAM

REQUIEM FOR MY FATHER

Never again to hear his voice,
Never to feel his touch,
To see the sweetness of his smile,
He whom I loved so much.

Such paltry things the words I pen
To speak my feelings here,
When he who was the best of men
Has left this mortal sphere.

Father, Grandfather and Great,
Brother and Uncle too.
All of us have felt the warmth
Of the love he gave us true.

Jack Blane

After war's terror he treasured
His family for all of his life:
But more than any, and always,
His "Darling," Kitty his wife.

No plaster saint, not perfect he
But caring, warm and kind.
This was him still when, ready to die,
He bade us not to mind.

Meaning so much to so many,
Always so ready to give,
He leaves a legacy of love
And forever in hearts will he live.

Yet his absence leaves a yawning void.
The world it shines less bright
Since my dearly belovèd father
Went into that dark night.

Jean Flannery 2013

A MISCELLANY

PICTURE GALLERY

This is "Uncle Hugh Millar drowned," according to the caption. We have a record of his birth but beyond the age of 8 he is a real mystery.

We also have women who are a mystery. Who is beautiful "Aunt Jenny?"

This picture was taken in Wick, Scotland. It was captioned as Jack's Great Great Grandparents but the photograph appears to be of a later date.

Margaret Elizabeth Millar around 1860
Jack's Great Grandmother

John and Margaret Elizabeth Millar
Jack's Great Grandparents in later life

Margaret Elizabeth Millar

I believe this to be a death photograph of Elizabeth, Jack's grandmother, a memento mori for her grieving Victorian mother.

> **BUCKINGHAMSHIRE COUNTY MUSEUM**
>
> Church Street, Aylesbury, Bucks. HP20 2QP
> Tel. Aylesbury 82158 and 88849
>
> Milton Keynes Archaeology Unit,
> 16 Erica Road, Stacey Bushes, Milton Keynes, Bucks. MK12 6PA Tel. Milton Keynes 312475
> Milton Keynes Exhibition Gallery,
> 555 Silbury Boulevard, Central Milton Keynes, Bucks. MK9 3HL Tel. Milton Keynes 605536
>
> ACQUISITION/TRANSFER OF TITLE FORM: 0074
>
> The Museum gratefully acknowledges the acquisition into the collection of the item(s) described below from the depositor.
>
> Depositor: Mr. J. BLANE Tel. no. 0234-768105
> Address: 199 Wavell Close, Stewartby, MK43 9LW, BEDFORD
>
> Owner: as above Tel. no.
> Address:
>
> Copyright Holder (if applicable): Tel. no.
> Address:
>
> Entry Form No.: Accession No.:
>
> Description: Beadwork valence made by female prisoners in Aylesbury Prison for donor's grandmother, Mary Elizabeth Powell, died 20 Oct. 1899.
>
> One photograph of Gt. Hampden teachers 1898 borrowed for copying – to be returned.
>
> Method of acquisition: (Donation) Purchase Bequest Long-term loan Other

Jack displays the beadwork valance. It has a design in shades of blue, bordered in yellow, and with white hanging strands.

"Aunt Sarah, Brentford."

She is Sarah Elizabeth Miller, born 1889, and a cousin to May.

"Sidney at Potton."
He may be Sidney Twinn who in 1914 joined the Suffolk Regiment, then transferred to the Royal Fusiliers before being invalided out of the army.

The Wisconsin, Guion Line mail steamer that took Henry Norman Powell from Liverpool to New York, arriving June 1882 after between 6 and 12 weeks at sea.

Advertisement for the Guion Line service.

Jean Blane Flannery

"Little Dolly Millar"
Elizabeth's daughter May, Jack's Mother
Photo mid to late 1880s

A teenage May Elizabeth Margaret Fraser Powell

15 February 1904

Marriage of Charles Henry Blane
and
May Elizabeth Margaret Fraser Powell

Back from left Charles' sisters: Alice, Eliza, Bessie
Back centre: May's grandmother Millar (Miller)
Back right: Charles' sister Jane and her husband
Front either side of Charles and May:
Charles' parents, Jane and Charles Blain (now Blane)

It's interesting how name spellings change!

May and Charles Henry Blane

The baby is most likely their eldest child, another Charles Henry, born 13 May 1905.

Young boys Martin (left) and Jack, on a rare visit to the seaside.

The Blane Family
Back: Henry, Jack, Charles, Don, Bob, Bernard
Front seated: Margaret, Parents, Martin
Not forgetting Patch the dog!

Outside the Bletchley Works Office, 1939
Note it has dropped the Forders name by now.

Walking out with his darling Kitty

New Recruit Jack

9 October 1940: Jack and Kitty's wedding
Back: Nellie, Reg, Jack's father Charles Henry
Front: Jack's mother May, Jack, Kitty, Kitty's mother Bertha

Martin, Edna, Jack, Kitty, Mary, Bernard
Front: Brenda
(Jack's brothers Martin and Bernard, Kitty's sisters-in-law Edna and Mary, and her sister Annie's daughter Brenda)

Jean Blane Flannery

The happy couple

On leave in 1941: fishing the 1st field of the Angling Club's water, at Stoke.

Not all the work was in the hospital!
5 June 1942

Break for a photo opportunity?

3 CCS Members
Jack back row, 2nd from left
21 September 1942 Jerusalem
Courtyard of Church of St Anne

Temple area, Mosque of Omar in the background.
Also 21 September 1942 on the same visit
Jack front row, 3rd from right.

But there were always good friends...
Jack seated behind front row

Brussels 6 September 1944
From left: Ginger, Derrick, Jack

Easter 1945, Jack meets daughter Jean

1946: We're bunching up primroses in the Cambridge Street garden with Nellie and Reg

Later in 1946: with Kitty and Jean
Wearing his "demob" suit
Cambridge Street

1959
Fisherman weighs his catch as Carole looks on

Setting the table for Christmas tea

Christmas 1959
Back: Reg, Jack, Nellie, Kitty
Front: Carole and Ken

Nellie was Kitty's older sister, Reg her husband, and Ken is their son.

Kitty moved to live with Nellie and Reg when she left school. After marriage, Kitty stayed with them and she and Jack lived there after the war until 1948, when they moved into their own home.

A keen eye watches Ken and Carole

On Holiday

Retirement presentation

Gathered to wish Jack well

On our family narrowboat holiday 1984

Bring on the rain! It couldn't dampen Jack's spirits.

1989: Family at Haslingfield, where Charles Henry Blane was born.
Left to right
Back: Katheryn (Martin's daughter), Martin, Jack
Front: Bob, Cousin Freda, Martin's wife Gwen, Kitty, Bernard's wife Daisy, Freda's husband Roy
Seated on ground: Bernard

Ready for their first Airship Flight 26 June 1990

50 Years Married 9 October 1990

Jack Blane

NORTH BEDFORDSHIRE AGE CONCERN
HANDICRAFT EXHIBITION
(FOR THE OVER FIFTIES)

FIRST PRIZE

SECTION.......... STUFFED TOYS.

AWARDED TO.......... MR. J. BLANE.

DATE 23rd April, 1994. SECRETARY *Elizabeth Stevens*

Just a small selection of the toys Jack made

2009
Conducting as we sang "Happy Birthday!"

NOW FOR THE FAMILY!

Family Foursome 2001
Kitty, Jean, Carole, Jack

Last picture of my children Winn, Kathryn and Carl all together. Mum and Dad's Diamond Anniversary celebration, 2000. Their appearance has changed some in the past 20 years - but not too much!

Carole's daughters, Dawn and Claire, 2012.
They still look about the same!

Carl's sons Bryce and Loren, 2018

Kathryn's children, 2012
Shannon at back, Ryan, Caitlin and Luke.
They have changed quite a bit since!

Dawn's children 2013
Oli (Oliver), Kitty and Toby.
They have certainly changed too.

Claire's sons William and cheeky Orin 2015
Another two who have changed more than a bit.

2005 and a big family anniversary party at Stewartby Club

It was a wonderful celebration of 65 years of happy marriage.

Enjoying the sun on the bench outside their bungalow.

After the final move into Salvete Care Home.
Kitty remained Jack's "Darling" right to the end of his life.

Carole reads the Queen's Platinum Anniversary card.
Family share in the celebration.

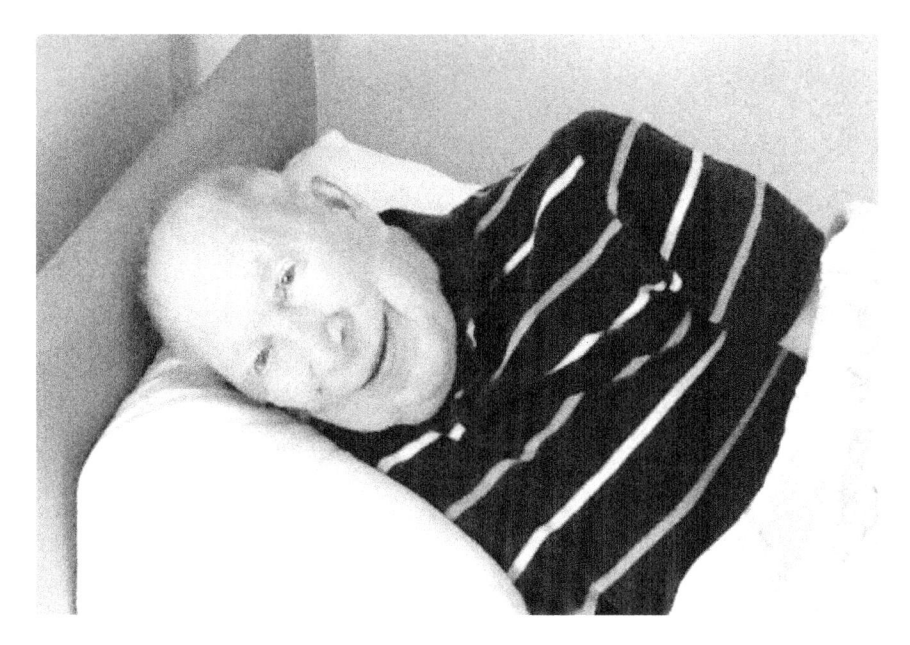

Content now just to stay in bed.

Family and friends had gathered to bid Jack farewell.
21 December 2012

FAMILY MYTHS

My father mentioned my paternal great grandfather, Henry Norman Powell, in the first chapter of this book. And I said that he was another story.

In fact there are two family myths concerning him. The first is that he had indeed died before his wife, leaving her a widow. The other is this. There seem to be some variations but the version I recall goes as follows.

Henry Powell, who was a ship's steward on the Atlantic run, was shipwrecked off the coast of North America in the early 1880s. He stayed in the USA where he moved to San Antonio, Texas, and wrote letter after letter to his wife Elizabeth, asking her to bring their young daughter and join him.

The story goes on to say that Elizabeth's parents intercepted Henry's letters, as they didn't want to lose her and their granddaughter.

Eventually, in desperation Henry wrote to the local vicar to ask his help, not even knowing if his wife was still alive. Alas that letter arrived too late, only shortly before Elizabeth did die. This really was a sad tale.

We know that both these stories are false. My very good friend Bev, a family historian, discovered the truth for us.

Henry did settle in the USA and did live in San Antonio, Texas.

That is where myth meets fact. And he may have initially written to his wife.

Her parents may have intercepted his letters, easy to do with Elizabeth working away and only home sporadically. They may even have told Henry that Elizabeth had died and/or Elizabeth that her husband had died. We shall never know.

What we do know is that Henry, under the name Harry Norman Powell (Harry being an early diminutive of Henry), made a bigamous marriage to Annie Austin Chalkley in Bexar County, Texas, in 1891.

I don't know when or how family members in the UK learned that Henry had remarried (though not that the second marriage was prior to Elizabeth's death). They may not have known until one of his sons got in touch to tell them Henry had died.

That part of the story also remains a mystery, as does how the US side of the family learned where to contact the UK branch. Perhaps they had even been in touch much earlier.

There is a story that Henry sent his young daughter May a coral necklace from the USA - but again, I frustratingly know no more.

I had also been under the impression that Henry was Welsh. But I have discovered that was also a myth, as he was born in London. However, Powell is a Welsh name so there is that ancestry.

As for Uncle Hugh Millar, we have no idea whether him having drowned is myth or fact!

But another family myth concerning Henry's first wife, my Great Grandmother Elizabeth, evidently grew up among the younger generation of family members.

One of them contacted me regarding the family tree. He believed that, as Elizabeth had died in Aylesbury Women's Prison, she had been an inmate there.

He wondered if I knew for what crime she had been imprisoned. That made me smile. Elizabeth was in fact a Prison Matron (Warden), as my father stated.

FAMILY FACTS

BLANE

For over 300 years all the Blane family members (in their various spellings) were born and lived in the mainly agricultural area around Sandy, in Bedfordshire.

The first of whom we have record is Robert Blayne. He died in 1584, aged 49 years. His occupation is given as Husbandman, which could be a free tenant farmer or a small landowner.

John Blain, born 1697, was a Gardener-yeoman. A yeoman was a land owner of higher social status than a husbandman. His is the first generation where the surname has changed from Blayne to Blain.

The occupation of William Blain, born 1809, is given as Agricultural Labourer in the 1861 Sandy Census, as is that of his son Charles, born 1845. Charles was born Blain, christened Blaine.

Then in 1868 Charles married Jane Twinn, who was born in Duxford, Cambridgeshire, some 20 miles from Sandy. In the 1851 census her father Henry's occupation is given as Jobber and Innkeeper.

Charles and Jane moved between Haslingfield, Cambridgeshire, where Charles Henry was born, and Potton in the Sandy area. They finally settled in Barton, Cambridgeshire, sometime between the years of 1881 and 1883.

Charles Henry was the first member of the family to be given and use only the surname Blane. His father was also only using that spelling by the time of Charles Henry's marriage.

In Barton, in the 1901 census (as in those of 1881 and 1891 in Haslingfield), Charles' occupation is given as Railway Platelayer. Charles Henry's is now given as Engine Cleaner.

By 1904, when he married May and was working on the Aylesbury to Cheddington line, Charles Henry had been promoted to Fireman.

His address at the time of his marriage was that of Margaret and May. It's possible he lodged with them at 46 Park Street when he went to work in Aylesbury, sometime after the 1901 census. However it happened, it's in Aylesbury that he met May.

Charles and May's eldest child, another Charles Henry, was born in Aylesbury in 1905. Their second child Henry James was born in Bletchley in 1907.

It was sometime between those two events, that Charles and May moved from Aylesbury to Bletchley with May's grandmother Margaret.

There they moved into a small house on Railway Terrace, where they lived until 1913. Margaret was the first of their children to be born at 14 Brooklands Road, in 1914, followed by Bernard, Jack and Martin.

It's interesting to note that in the census of 1911 the registration district is Fenny Stratford, at that time the larger town, with

Bletchley a smaller satellite.

Charles Henry's occupation is given as Engine Stoker (Fireman). It was later that he became a First-class Driver on the Bletchley to London (Euston) line.

The house on Brooklands Road was Charles and May's final home, where they lived for many years. Charles Henry died there in 1956, of myeloid leukaemia.

May continued to live in the house with her youngest son Martin until she moved into assisting living in the 1960s, eventually dying in Renny Lodge hospital in 1971. The cause of death was given as bronchopneumonia.

FRASER/MILLAR

Margaret Fraser (Frazer) was born in Claymoss in the parish of Dyke, Morayshire, in a small single storey thatched dwelling house near the sea, 30 September 1828.

Her father was William Fraser, born in 1793 in Muirtown, Dyke, Morayshire. It was a settlement of 4 houses and now only exists as the name of a wood near Dyke. He married her mother, Marjory (May) Young, in 1816.

The family members were known as the Frasers of Claymoss. They were still living there at least up until the First World War.

What is certain is that by 1935 all the Frasers had left and sadly Claymoss as a house doesn't seem to exist anymore. However the fields around it are still called Claymoss.

Margaret Fraser married John Millar, who was born in Cupar, Fife. He worked as a Flour Miller in Dyke.

Their daughter Elizabeth Millar was born 15 June 1855, in a dwelling house at Moy Mills that was attached to the mill (presumably where her father worked) at Dyke. On her birth certificate it is noted that there was another girl, deceased, but with no further details.

Both John and Hugh were born in Edinburgh, Hugh in 1863. We don't know in just what year the family moved to England. However, in the 1871 census the family is recorded as living in Belper, Derbyshire. John and Margaret must have moved the family to Belper by 1869, as their youngest child Robert was born there in that year. John was working as a Flour Miller Foreman.

We have no record of Hugh after this census.

By 1881 the family had moved to London. John, whose occupation is given as Miller (Corn), worked in a mill about 100 doors from their home, both being on Rotherhithe Street.

Although we don't know when Elizabeth started to work at Woking Women's Prison, she was certainly there from 1881 when she was an Assistant Warden. May was living with her grandparents, John and Margaret.

John Millar died sometime between 1891, when his occupation is given as Miller of Wheat and Corn, and 1901. The women probably moved to Aylesbury, perhaps after John died, in 1898. That is when the reference you will see for May was written.

Elizabeth died in the hospital of Aylesbury Women's Prison, where she was working as Matron (Warden), in 1899. Although Elizabeth died of peritonitis, what caused that isn't recorded.

The young daughter of Margaret's son John, another Elizabeth, was staying with Margaret and May in Aylesbury at the time of the 1901 census. May's occupation is given there as school teacher, so we know she was still working at the time. Her Uncle John's occupation is given as Engine Driver.

1911 is currently the last publicly available census for England and Wales. The 1921 census will be in the public domain in 2022.

POWELL

The Powell family lived in Surrey from at least 1738. The first member of whom we have any record is William Powell, born in Burwood.

Thomas Powell was born in Horley, Surrey, in 1837. His son Henry Norman Powell was born in 1856 in Norwood, then still a town in Surrey prior to it being engulfed by Greater London.

By 1881 Thomas is listed as a builder in the Lee, London, Census. The family must have been quite well to do as Thomas and his wife Mary had a live-in servant, Lavinia Lamb, a widow aged 55.

Henry married Elizabeth Millar in Stepney, London, in 1877. Their only daughter, May Elizabeth Margaret Fraser Millar, was born in 1878. Her given names clearly reflect her heritage.

Although we have a record of Elizabeth in the 1881 census, we could find none of Henry.

Henry did enter the USA as an immigrant in June 1882. He had a paid passage from Liverpool (in Steerage) on the mail ship Wisconsin, a single screw steamer. On the ship's list his occupation is listed as Lab^r (labourer).

His name is simply given as Hy Powell on the ship's passenger list and the immigration document. In all further documentation he is known by the diminutive Harry, which was commonly used for Henry.

Henry married Annie A Chalkley in Bexar County, Texas, 5 December 1891. In the 1910 census his occupation is given as Marine Engineer. He lived in San Antonio, Texas, at least from then until his death in 1932.

We know the names of two sons and a daughter, and those of three grandsons. His children are named in the obituary. His grandsons were:

Harry Charles Powell, 29 December 1917 - 19 October 1969
Thomas Austin Powell 29 August 1921 - 5 January 1997
James E (Blackie) Powell 22 November 1926 - 31 December 2012

However, that's where our knowledge of this branch of the family ends. I did find Harry/Henry's grave online.

It is in St Mary's Catholic Church Cemetery, in San Antonio.

His birth year on the gravestone is a year out, as is that of his wife Annie, who died in 1930, on hers.

Their newspaper obituaries also both contain various errors.

OBITUARY

San Antonio Express
February 16, 1932

Funeral services for Harry N. Powell, 76, for 25 years a San Antonio resident, who died Monday will be held Tuesday at the residence, 1110 Lee Hall Street, to be followed by requiem mass at St. Anne's church with Rev. Feeney officiating.

Pallbearers will be C.O. Hill, A.W. Chalkley, H.J. Dalton, Louis Sammer, T.M. Little, Jr., and C.J. Salme.

Powell was a native of London England, and had lived in the United States the past 60 (*50*) years. Surviving him are a daughter, Mrs. O.A. (*Vera*) Thompson of Hebbronville, and two sons, Harry C. Powell of San Francisco, Cal., and William E. Powell of San Antonio.

DEATH CERTIFICATE

Date of birth (*christening*): December 25, 1856
Residence: 1110 Lee Hall, San Antonio, Tx
Occupation: retired
Cause of death: mycarditis (*sic*)

FAMILY RECORDS

Note: Those who wrote and transcribed records frequently used their own spellings.

Claymoss - historic description

26/09/1793 FRASER, WILLIAM (Old Parish Registers Births 133/ 30 244 Dyke) Page 244 of 396
©Crown copyright, National Records of Scotland. Image was generated at 07 February 2021 14:25

Birth record of William Fraser 1793

28/09/1828 FRASER, MARGARET (Old Parish Registers Births 133/ 50 37 Dyke) Page 37 of 180
©Crown copyright, National Records of Scotland. Image was generated at 07 February 2021 12:20

Birth record of Margaret Fraser 1828

Jean Blane Flannery

1855 MILLAR, ELIZABETH (Statutory registers Births 133/ 14)
©Crown copyright, National Records of Scotland. Image was generated at 07 February 2021 11:43

Birth record of Elizabeth Millar 1855

William Blane
England and Wales Census, 1861

Tools

Name:	William Blane
Event Type:	Census
Event Date:	1861
Event Place:	Sandy, Bedfordshire, England, United Kingdom
Event Place (Original):	Sandy, Bedfordshire, England
County:	Bedfordshire
Parish:	Sandy
Registration District:	Biggleswade
Residence Note:	Girtford Village
Sex:	Male
Age:	51
Marital Status:	Married
Occupation:	Agricultural Labourer
Birth Year (Estimated):	1810
Birthplace:	Sandy, Bedfordshire
Relationship to Head of Household:	Head
Relationship to Head of Household	Head

Household	Role	Sex	Age	Birthplace
William Blane	Head	Male	51	Sandy, Bedfordshire
Mary Blane	Wife	Female	54	..., Bedfordshire
Eliza Blane	Daughter	Female	20	Girtford, Bedfordshire
Louisa Blane	Daughter	Female	14	Girtford, Bedfordshire
Charles Blane	Son	Male	17	Girtford, Bedfordshire

William Blain Household
1861 Census, Sandy

John Millar
England and Wales Census, 1871

Name:	John Millar
Event Type:	Census
Event Date:	1871
Event Place:	Belper, Derbyshire, England, United Kingdom
Event Place (Original):	Belper, Derbyshire, England
Sub-District:	Belper
Enumeration District:	3
Sex:	Male
Age:	40
Marital Status:	Married
Occupation:	Flour Miller Foreman
Birth Year (Estimated):	1831
Birthplace:	Scotland
Relationship to Head of Household:	Head
Relationship to Head of Household (Original):	Head
Affiliate Image Identifier:	GBC/1871/3582/0069

Household	Role	Sex	Age	Birthplace
John Millar	Head	Male	40	Scotland
Elizabeth Millar	Wife	Female	43	Scotland
Elizabeth Millar	Daughter	Female	15	Scotland
John Millar	Son	Male	12	Scotland
Hugh Millar	Son	Male	8	Scotland
Robert Millar	Son	Male	2	Belper, Derbyshire

**John Millar Household
1871 Census
Belper, Derbyshire
Note: wife Elizabeth's first name is missing.**

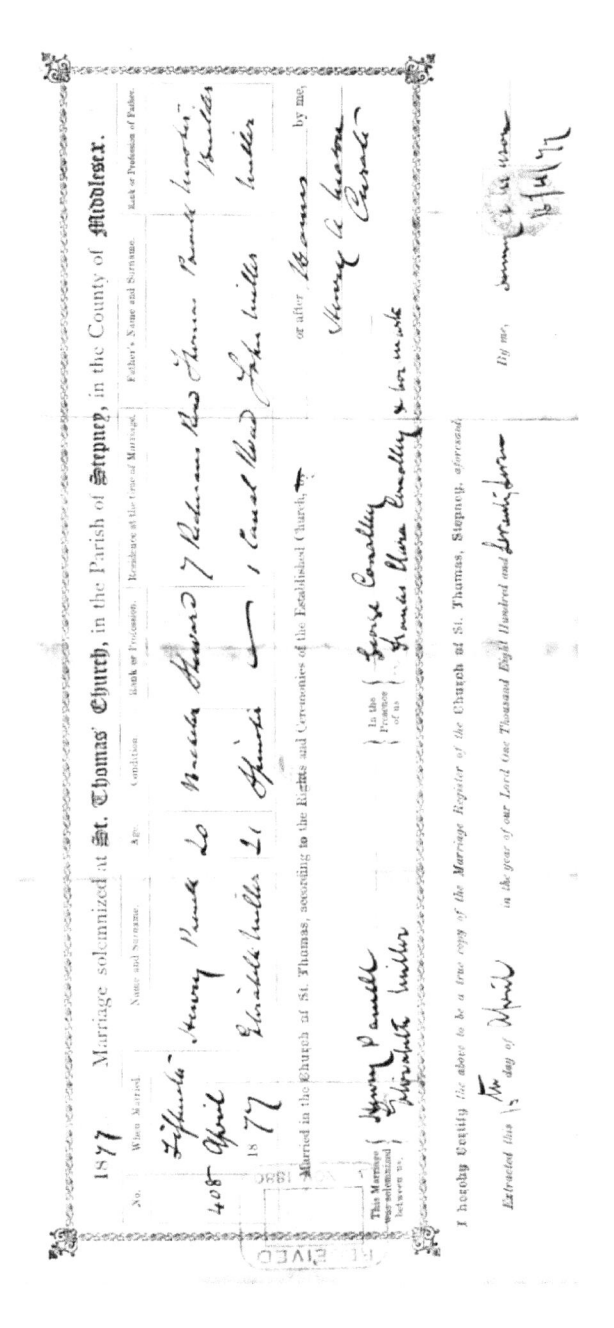

Marriage: Henry Powell and Elizabeth Miller 1877
Note: Henry's middle name, Norman, is missing

May Elizabeth Margaret Fraser Powell
Birth certificate 1878

John Millar
England and Wales Census, 1881

Tools

Name:	John Millar
Event Type:	Census
Event Date:	1881
Event Place:	Rotherhithe, London, Surrey, England
Registration District:	St Olave Southwark
Residence Note:	Rotherhithe Street
Sex:	Male
Age:	57
Marital Status:	Married
Marital Status (Original):	Married
Occupation:	Miller (Corn)
Birth Year (Estimated):	1824
Birthplace:	Scotland
Relationship to Head of Household:	Head
Page Number:	27
Registration Number:	RG11
Piece/Folio:	575/17

Household	Role	Sex	Age	Birthplace
John Millar	Head	Male	57	Scotland
Elizth Millar	Wife	Female	53	Scotland
John Millar	Son	Male	22	Scotland
Robt W Millar	Son	Male	12	Belper, Derbyshire, England
May E Powell	Grand Child	Female	0	Rothere, Surrey, England

John Millar Household, now without Hugh
1881 Census, London

Elizabeth Powell
England and Wales Census, 1881

Name:	Elizabeth Powell
Event Type:	Census
Event Date:	1881
Event Place:	Woking, Surrey, England
Registration District:	Guildford
Residence Note:	Knaphill Woking
Sex:	Female
Age:	26
Marital Status:	Widow
Marital Status (Original):	Widow
Occupation:	Assistant Matron
Birth Year (Estimated):	1855
Birthplace:	Moray, Scotland
Relationship to Head of Household:	Officer
Page Number:	3
Registration Number:	RG11
Piece/Folio:	773/97

Elizabeth Powell
1881 Census
Working in Woking Prison

Charles Blane
England and Wales Census, 1881

Tools

Name:	Charles Bane
Event Type:	Census
Event Date:	1881
Event Place:	Haslingfield, Cambridgeshire, England
Registration District:	Chesterton
Residence Note:	Cantaloupe Road
Sex:	Male
Age:	38
Marital Status:	Married
Marital Status (Original):	Married
Occupation:	Railway Platelayer
Birth Year (Estimated):	1843
Birthplace:	Sandy, Bedfordshire, England
Relationship to Head of Household:	Head
Page Number:	31
Registration Number:	RG11
Piece/Folio:	1662/89

Household	Role	Sex	Age	Birthplace
Charles Blane	Head	Male	38	Sandy, Bedfordshire, England
Jane Blane	Wife	Female	36	Duxford, Cambridgeshire, England
Henry Blane	Son	Male	11	Potton, Bedfordshire, England
Arthur Blane	Son	Male	9	Potton, Bedfordshire, England
Jane Blane	Daughter	Female	5	Potton, Bedfordshire, England
Bessie Blane	Daughter	Female	2	Potton, Bedfordshire, England

Charles Blain Household
1881 Census, Haslingfield

The name of Charles Henry is missing from this census. It appears from other records that he was born 11 July 1881.

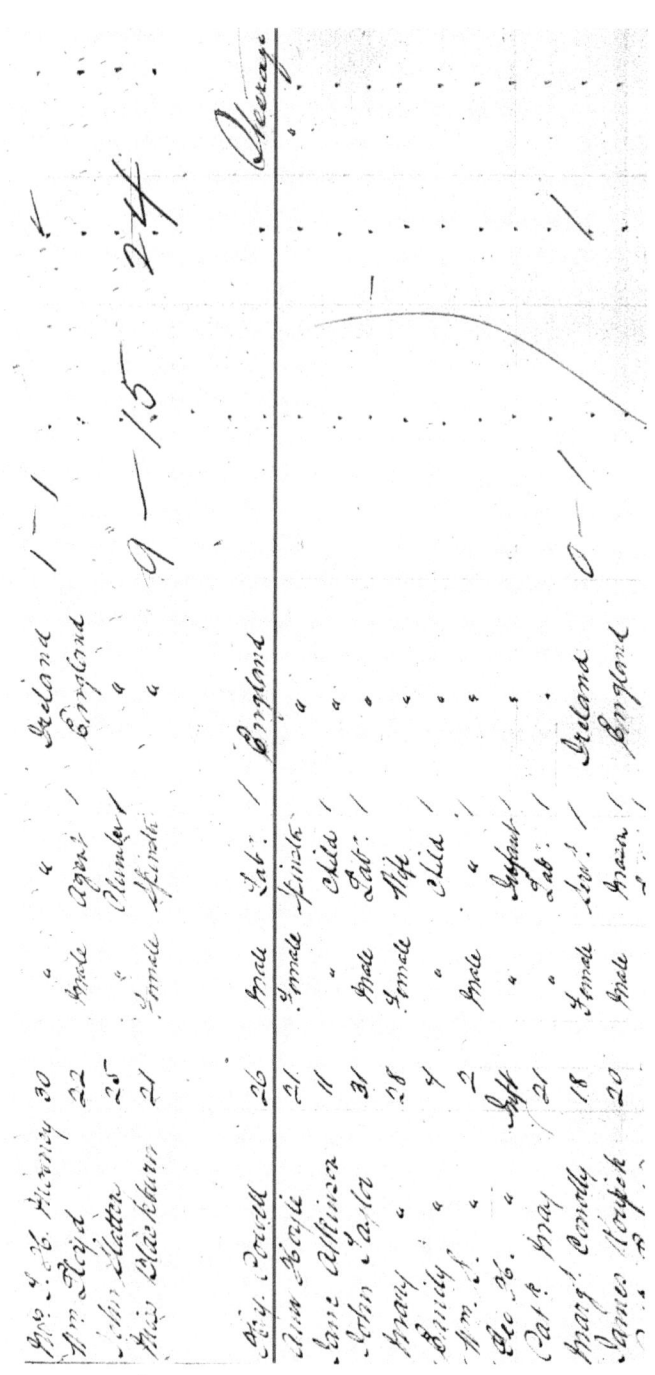

Henry/Harry Powell's Immigration Record
Original 1882

Jack Blane

Hy Powell
New York Passenger Lists

Name	**Hy Powell**
Event Type	Immigration
Event Date	1882
Event Place	New York City, New York, United States
Gender	Male
Age	26
Birth Year (Estimated)	1856
Birthplace	England
Ship Name	Wisconsin

Henry/Harry Powell
Transcript of Immigration Record

John Miller
England and Wales Census, 1891

Name:	John Miller
Event Type:	Census
Event Date:	1891
Event Place:	Rotherhithe, Southwark, London, England, United Kingdom
Event Place (Original):	Rotherhithe, London, England
Event Place Note:	Rotherhithe Street
County:	London
Parish:	Rotherhithe
Ecclesiastical Parish:	ST MARYS
Enumeration District:	1
Registration District:	St Olave Southwark
Sex:	Male
Age:	61
Marital Status:	Married
Occupation:	Miller Wheat & C
Birth Year (Estimated):	1830
Birthplace:	Fifeshire, Scotland
Relationship to Head of Household:	Head
Page Number:	17
Registration Number:	RG12
Piece/Folio:	381/ 12
Affiliate Record Type:	Household
Affiliate Image Identifier:	GBC/1891/0381/0025&parentid=GBC/1891/0003220866

Household	Role	Sex	Age	Birthplace
John Miller	Head	Male	61	Fifeshire, Scotland
Margaret E Miller	Wife	Female	63	Fifeshire, England
May Marget Elizt Powell	Granddaughter	Female	13	London, England
Henry Dunklin	Lodger	Male	25	England

John Miller Household
1891 Census, London

Charles Blane
England and Wales Census, 1891

Tools

Name:	Charles Blane
Event Type:	Census
Event Date:	1891
Event Place:	Barton, Cambridgeshire, England, United Kingdom
Event Place (Original):	Barton, Cambridgeshire, England
Event Place Note:	Long Road
County:	Cambridgeshire
Parish:	Barton
Ecclesiastical Parish:	BARTON
Enumeration District:	8
Registration District:	Chesterton
Sex:	Male
Age:	46
Marital Status:	Married
Occupation:	Platelayer
Birth Year (Estimated):	1845
Birthplace:	Girtford, Bedfordshire, England
Relationship to Head of Household:	Head
Page Number:	24
Registration Number:	RG12
Piece/Folio:	1282/149
Affiliate Record Type:	Household
Affiliate Image Identifier:	GBC/1891/1282/0299&parentid=GBC/1891/0009534143

Household	Role	Sex	Age	Birthplace
Charles Blane	Head	Male	46	Girtford, Bedfordshire, England
Jane Blane	Wife	Female	44	Duxford, Cambridgeshire, England
Henry Blane	Son	Male	21	Polton, Bedfordshire, England
Bessie Blane	Daughter	Female	12	Polton, Bedfordshire, England
Charles Blane	Son	Male	9	Haslingfield, Cambridgeshire, England
Alice Blane	Daughter	Female	7	Barton, Cambridgeshire, England
Eliza Blane	Daughter	Female	5	Barton, Cambridgeshire, England

Charles Blain/Blane Household
1891 Census, Barton
Note: Charles Henry's middle name omitted.

TESTIMONIALS TO MAY ELIZABETH M F BLANE

CHRIST CHURCH SCHOOL, PARADISE STREET 1897
Letter 1

Ch. Ch. Vicarage,
Rotherhithe, S.E.

19 Jan. 1897.

I have much pleasure in certifying that Miss May E.M.F. Powell has served her four years apprenticeship in our National Infants School, and that during that time her conduct was always most exemplary. I consider her to be a young woman of high moral & Christian character, most conscientious, painstaking, industrious & kind to the children, & can strongly recommend her for some higher position in Town or country School. (Signed) J. Martyn Baysley
Vicar of Ch. Ch. Rotherhithe
& Chairman of Managers of the Ch. Ch. Rotherhithe Nat. Schs.

CHRIST CHURCH SCHOOL, PARADISE STREET 1897
Letter 2

Miss M. Cowell has served her apprenticeship in Christ Church Infants' School, Paradise Street, Rotherhithe.

I have always found her a very successful, conscientious and energetic teacher.

She understands her work in every branch including Kindergarten, Tonic-sol-fa, & Musical Drill.

She is a good deep linguist and gentle in manner.

Of her personal character I can also speak in the highest praise.

Signed Louise Chudleigh
Head Mistress
Ch. Ch. Infants' Sch.
Paradise St.
Rotherhithe.

January 23rd 1897.

HAMPDEN NATIONAL SCHOOL LETTER 1898
Page 1

Oct. 11. 1898.

I have much pleasure in certifying that Miss May Powell faithfully performed her duties as Assistant Mistress (Art. 60.) in the Hampden National School during the year she occupied that position, commencing Sep. 13th 1897 and ending Sep. 13th 1898.

The managers were obliged to make a change in the staff so as to enable the Head Mistress of the School if possible to have a permanent companion to live with her in the School

HAMPDEN NATIONAL SCHOOL LETTER 1898
Page 2

House, and to raise the position of two monitresses who had worked for a long time in the school — They were always fully satisfied with Miss Powell's work —

Alfred Marshall
Correspondent of Hampden National School
Rector of Great & Little Hampden

HAMPDEN NATIONAL SCHOOL REFERENCE 1898
Page 1

Cross Street
National Schools
Cowes
I. W.

Sep: 28th 1898

I have only known Miss May Powell for three months, but I am pleased to be able to speak very highly of her.

I have always found her industrious, pleasant & obliging –

HAMPDEN NATIONAL SCHOOL REFERENCE 1898
Page 2

While engaged in the Great Hampden National School, Miss Powell was responsible for the Infants & the results of her work were gratifying –

I feel sure wherever she is appointed she will give satisfaction –

      E. M. Coney.
        Certifd. Tch:

DEATH AND FUNERAL OF A PRISON OFFICIAL.— The death of Mrs. Powell, matron of H.M. Convict Prison at Aylesbury, occurred on Friday last, and on Wednesday the remains of the deceased lady were interred in the Aylesbury Cemetery. The service was conducted by the Rev. J. Knight-Newton, (prison chaplain), and the coffin was borne to its last resting place by warders from the prison. About forty of the prison officials followed the deceased, these including the governor.

Elizabeth Powell local newspaper report 1899

Elizabeth Millar
England and Wales Census, 1901

Tools

Name:	Elizabeth Millar
Event Type:	Census
Event Date:	31 Mar 1901
Event Place:	Aylesbury, Buckinghamshire, England, United Kingdom
County:	Buckinghamshire
Civil Parish:	Aylesbury
Ecclesiastical Parish:	Aylesbury St Mary & St John
Sub-District:	Aylesbury
Registration District:	Aylesbury
Sex:	Female
Age:	77
Occupation:	NO OCCUPATION
Relationship to Head of Household:	Head
Birth Year (Estimated):	1824
Birthplace:	Scotland
Schedule Type:	257
Page Number:	39

Household	Role	Sex	Age	Birthplace
Elizabeth Millar	Head	Female	77	Scotland
May Powell	Grand Daughter	Female	22	Rotherhithe, London
Elizabeth Millar	Grand Daughter	Female	12	Rotherhithe, London

Margaret Elizabeth Millar Household
1901 Census, Aylesbury
Note: Margaret's first name omitted.
May's occupation is given as School Teacher in this census.

Charles Blane
England and Wales Census, 1901

Name:	Charles Blane
Event Type:	Census
Event Date:	31 Mar 1901
Event Place:	Barton, Cambridgeshire, England, United Kingdom
County:	Cambridgeshire
Civil Parish:	Barton
Ecclesiastical Parish:	Barton St Peter
Sub-District:	Shelford
Registration District:	Chesterton
Sex:	Male
Age:	56
Occupation:	PLATELAYER ON RY
Relationship to Head of Household:	Head
Birth Year (Estimated):	1845
Birthplace:	Sandy, Bedfordshire
Schedule Type:	50
Page Number:	7

Household	Role	Sex	Age	Birthplace
Charles Blane	Head	Male	56	Sandy, Bedfordshire
Jane Blane	Wife	Female	54	Duxford, Cambridgeshire
Charles Blane	Son	Male	19	Haslingfield, Cambridgeshire
Eliza Blane	Daughter	Female	15	Barton, Cambridgeshire

Charles Blane Household
1901 Census, Barton
Note: Charles' middle name Henry omitted

Charles Blane
England and Wales Census, 1901

Tools

Name:	Charles Blane
Event Type:	Census
Event Date:	31 Mar 1901
Event Place:	Barton, Cambridgeshire, England, United Kingdom
County:	Cambridgeshire
Civil Parish:	Barton
Ecclesiastical Parish:	Barton St Peter
Sub-District:	Shelford
Registration District:	Chesterton
Sex:	Male
Age:	19
Occupation:	ENGINE CLEANER ON RY
Relationship to Head of Household:	Son
Birth Year (Estimated):	1882
Birthplace:	Haslingfield, Cambridgeshire
Schedule Type:	50
Page Number:	7

Household	Role	Sex	Age	Birthplace
Charles Blane	Head	Male	56	Sandy, Bedfordshire
Jane Blane	Wife	Female	54	Duxford, Cambridgeshire
Charles Blane	Son	Male	19	Haslingfield, Cambridgeshire
Eliza Blane	Daughter	Female	15	Barton, Cambridgeshire

Charles Henry Blane
1901 Census, Barton
Note: Charles' middle name Henry omitted

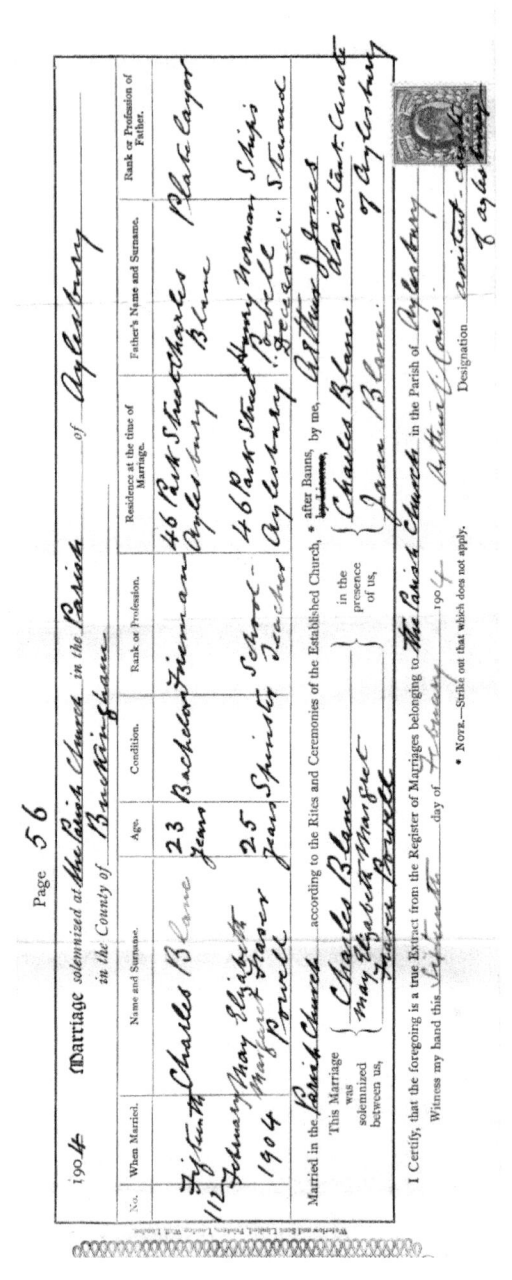

Marriage of Charles Henry Blane and
May Elizabeth Margaret Fraser Powell
Note: Charles' middle name Henry is missing here too.

Excerpts from a newspaper story of October 1904, involving Charles Henry Blane. At the time, Charles was fireman on the train that hit the deceased.

Suicide and attempted suicide were criminal acts, so suicide was not lightly given as cause of death.

CHEDDINGTON.

SAD FATALITY.

A MAN KILLED ON THE RAILWAY.

On Saturday evening Mr. E. Wilkins, Coroner, held an inquest at the Royal Bucks Hospital, Aylesbury, on the body of Stephen Turney, a platelayer, employed on the London and North-Western Railway, who is a Cheddington man, and has relatives living at Mentmore. Mr. Albert Cox was the Foreman of the Jury, and the London and North-Western Railway Company were represented by Inspectors Taylor and Gurney, and Mr. Chadwick, the station-master at Aylesbury.

Mrs. Elizabeth Edwards, wife of George Edwards, labourer, of Wing, said the body which the jury had just seen was that of her son, Stephen Turney, who was a platelayer in the employ of the L. and N.-W. Railway. He lived at Broughton, in the parish of Bierton, and was 21 years of age. Deceased lived in the house witness occupied until eight weeks ago, when she married again. Deceased had been in the employ of the Railway Company for three years.

Witness came to stay with deceased at Broughton on Thursday, as he thought of getting married in a day or two. On Thursday night he went out with Miss Edith Annie Hyde, the girl he was engaged to,

There had been no disagreement between her and deceased. Witness called deceased at about a quarter past five the previous morning, and got up and made him some tea. Deceased got up about a quarter to six, and left the house soon after six to go to work. They were very friendly when he left. Deceased's hearing was good, and he was not at all deaf. Witness next saw him in the hospital at about nine o'clock. She was present when he died at about ten o'clock on the previous morning. Whilst witness was with him he made no statement to her. He had never threatened to destroy himself. When he and Miss Hyde returned on Thursday night they appeared to be on good terms. Deceased said he was going to Aylesbury to work.

William Facer, gate-keeper on the railway at Broughton Crossing, spoke to finding deceased soon after seven o'clock the previous morning in the four-foot way about six hundred yards on the Aylesbury side of the crossing. When spoken to, he said "Kill me out of my misery, I'm sure I shall never get over this." No part of the body was on the line. Deceased was asked how it had come about, and he repled, "I'm sure I don't know."

Charles Blane, fireman, and Joseph Froodham, driver of the 7.5 train out of Aylesbury, gave formal evidence as to knocking something on the line near Broughton, and to finding flesh on the engine.

John Reid, foreman platelayer, also gave evidence.

Dr. Russell Edwards Palmer, house surgeon at the Royal Bucks. Hospital, Aylesbury, detailed the nature of the injuries, and said deceased was practically pulseless when brought to the Hospital; death was due to shock from the injuries received.

After the Coroner had summed up, the Jury returned a verdict to the effect that death was due to injuries received, but there was no evidence to show how deceased came under the train.

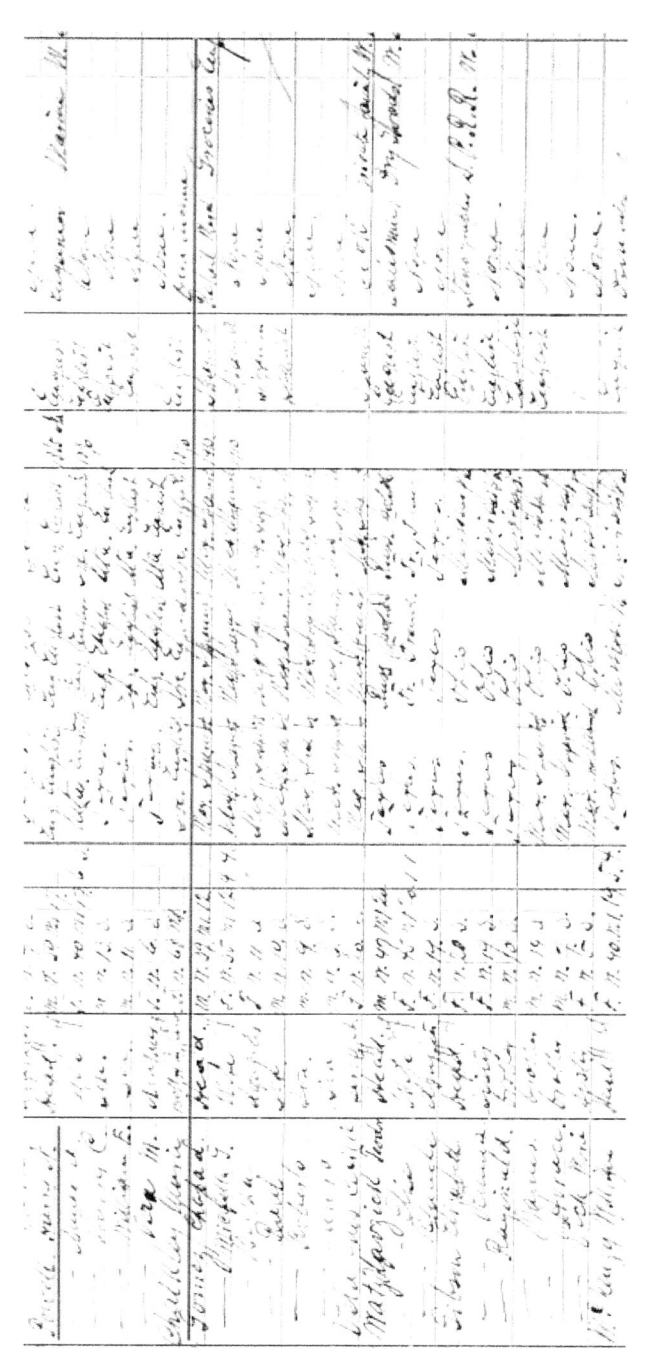

Harry Norman Powell Household
1910 Census, San Antonio, Texas

Jean Blane Flannery

Name:	Charles Henry Blane
Event Type:	Census
Event Date:	1911
Event Place:	Fenny Stratford, Buckinghamshire, England, United Kingdom
County:	Buckinghamshire
Parish:	Fenny Stratford
Sub-District:	Fenny Stratford
Sub-District Number:	1
District Number:	148
Enumeration District:	12
Registration District:	Newport Pagnell
Sex:	Male
Age:	29
Marital Status:	Married
Marital Status (Original):	MARRIED
Occupation:	RAILWAY ENGINE STOKER
Number in Family:	5
Birth Year (Estimated):	1882
Birthplace:	Haslingfield, Cambridgeshire
Relationship to Head of Household:	Head
Schedule Type:	37
Page Number:	1
Registration Number:	RG14
Piece/Folio:	75
Affiliate Record Identifier:	GBC/1911/RG14/07980/0075/1

Household	Role	Sex	Age	Birthplace
Charles Henry Blane	Head	Male	29	Haslingfield, Cambridgeshire
May Blane	Wife	Female	32	London Rotherhithe, London
Charles Henry Blane	Son	Male	6	Bucks Aylesbury, Buckinghamshire
Henry James Blane	Son	Male	4	Bucks Bletchley, Buckinghamshire
Donald Fraser Blane	Son	Male	2	Bucks Bletchley, Buckinghamshire
Margaret Millar	Grand Mother In Law	Female	84	Forres Resident, Morayshire

Charles Henry Blane Household
1911 Census, Fenny Stratford (Bletchley)

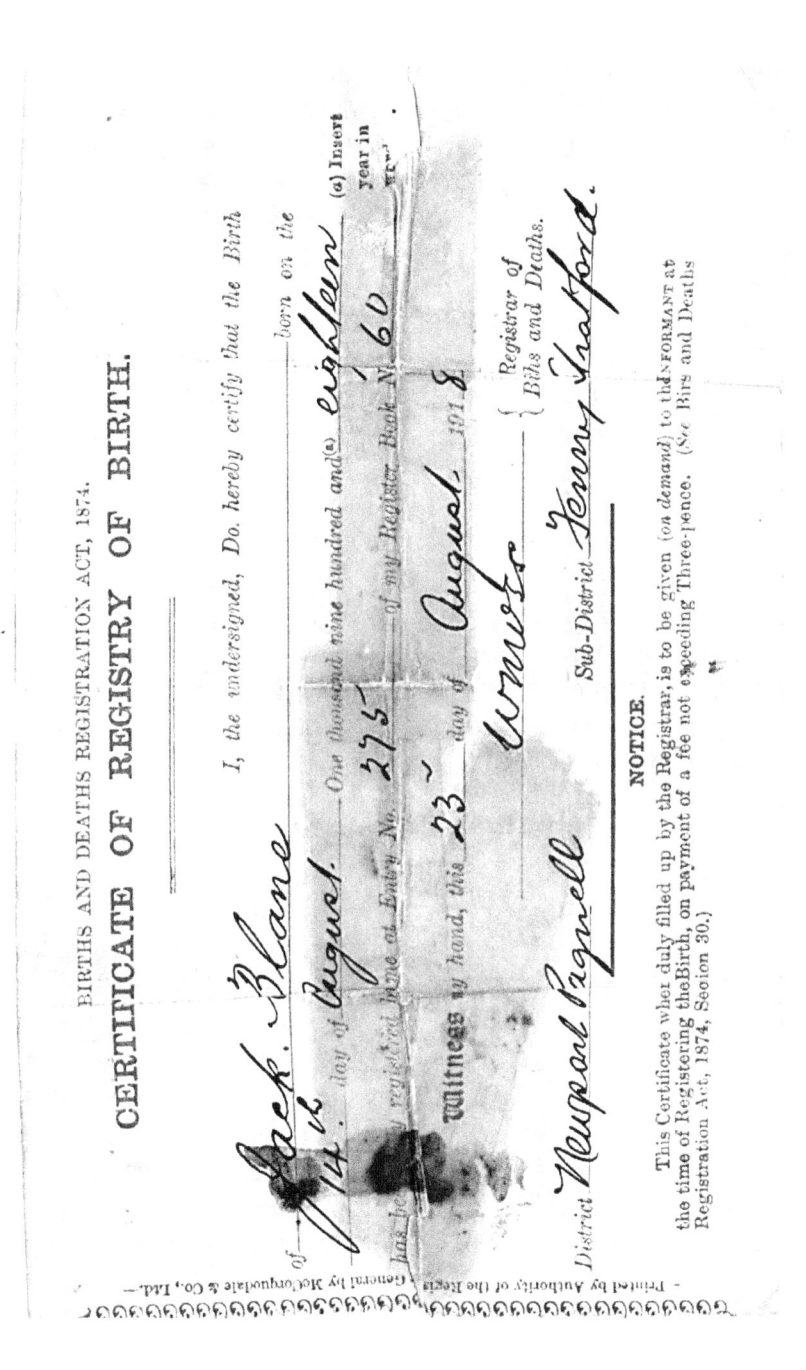

Jack Blane

Jack Blane Birth Certificate 1918

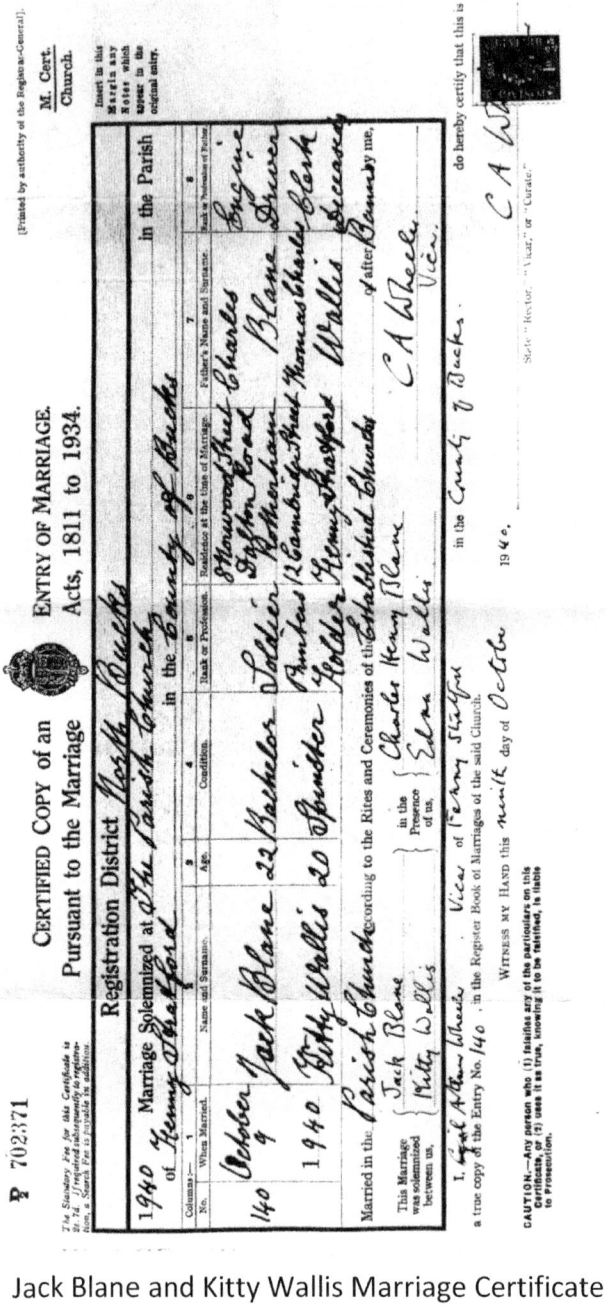

Jack Blane and Kitty Wallis Marriage Certificate
9 October 1940

MR. J. BLANE—MISS K. WALLIS.

Mr. Jack Blane, seventh son of Mr. and Mrs. C. H. Blane, of 14, Brooklands Road, Bletchley, and Miss Kitty Wallis, youngest daughter of the late Mr. Wallis and Mrs. T. C. Wallis, of Sheffield, were married in St. Martin's Church, Bletchley, on Wednesday. The bridegroom, who is in the Forces, was formerly employed by the London Brick Co. Ltd., and the bride is employed by the Premier Press.

The Rev. C. A. Wheeler (Vicar) officiated. Mr. R. G. Cutts (bride's brother-in-law) gave the bride away. She wore a dress of white broche taffeta over net, a head-dress and coronet of lilies and silver shoes and carried a bouquet of red roses. Her gift from the bridegroom was a string of pearls.

The maids of honour were Mrs. T. Wallis and Mrs. F. Wallis (the bride's sisters-in-law), who were attired in pale pink net and organdie over taffeta trimmed with blue velvet, shoulder length veils, coronets of pink leaves and roses and silver shoes. Each carried a bouquet of deep pink carnations. The bridegroom presented them with gold horseshoe brooches.

Little Brenda Gee (bride's niece) was bridesmaid. She wore a dress of pale blue net and organdie over taffeta trimmed with pale pink velvet, a Victorian bonnet in pink and blue taffeta, and carried a posy of Michaelmas daisies. The bridegroom gave her a gold bangle.

The page, Master Charles Wallis (bride's nephew), wore a blue pale satin outfit with white shoes, and the bridegroom gave him a regimental tie pin.

The bride's mother wore a navy blue dress and a hat to match, and the bridegroom's mother a petrel blue dress with hat and coat to tone. Mr. Martin Blane was best man and Mr. Bernard Blane groomsman.

Thirty guests attended the reception in St. Martin's Hall.

Several cheques, including one from the London Brick Co. employees, were among the 35 presents. The bride gave her husband a leather wallet and the bride received a cut glass salad bowl and cake knife from her colleagues at the Premier Press.

Local newspaper report of wedding

Jean Blane Flannery

MARRIAGE OF MR. JACK BLANE

The wedding took place at St. Martin's Church, Bletchley, on Wednesday, of Mr. Jack Blane, sixth son of Mr. and Mrs. C. Blane, of 14, Brooklands Rd., Bletchley, and Miss Kitty Wallis, youngest daughter of the late Mr. Wallis and Mrs. T. C. Wallis, of Sheffield. The Rev. C. A. Wheeler (Vicar) conducted the ceremony.

The bride, who was given away by her brother-in-law, Mr. R. Cutts, wore white broche taffeta over net, a head-dress and coronet of lilies, and silver shoes. Her bouquet consisted of red roses. The bride was attended by two maids-of-honour, Mrs. T. and Mrs. F. Wallis, a small bridesmaid, Miss Brenda Gee (niece of bride), and a page, Master Charles Wallis (bride's nephew). The maids of honour were attired in pale pink net and organdie over taffeta, shoulder length veils, with coronets of pink leaves and roses, and silver shoes. Their bouquets were of deep pink carnations. The small bridesmaid was dressed in pale blue net and organdie over taffeta, with Victorian bonnet in pink and blue taffeta. She carried a posy of Michaelmas daisies. Master Charles Wallis wore pale blue satin and white shoes. The bridegroom gave gold horseshoe brooches to the maids of honour, a gold bangle to the bridesmaid and a regimental tiepin to the page. The bride's gift to the bridegroom was a leather wallet and the groom's gift to the bride, a string of pearls.

Mr. Martin Blane (bridegroom's brother) was best man, and Mr. Bernard Blane was groomsman.

A reception held at St. Martin's Hall was attended by 30 guests.

Several cheques were among the 35 presents Mr. and Mrs. Blane received. The gifts also included a cut-glass salad bowl and cake knife from Premier Press Employees where the bride is employed, and a £3 cheque from London Brick Co. employees, where the bridegroom was employed before joining H.M. Forces. The bridegroom is on seven days' leave.

And from another local newspaper

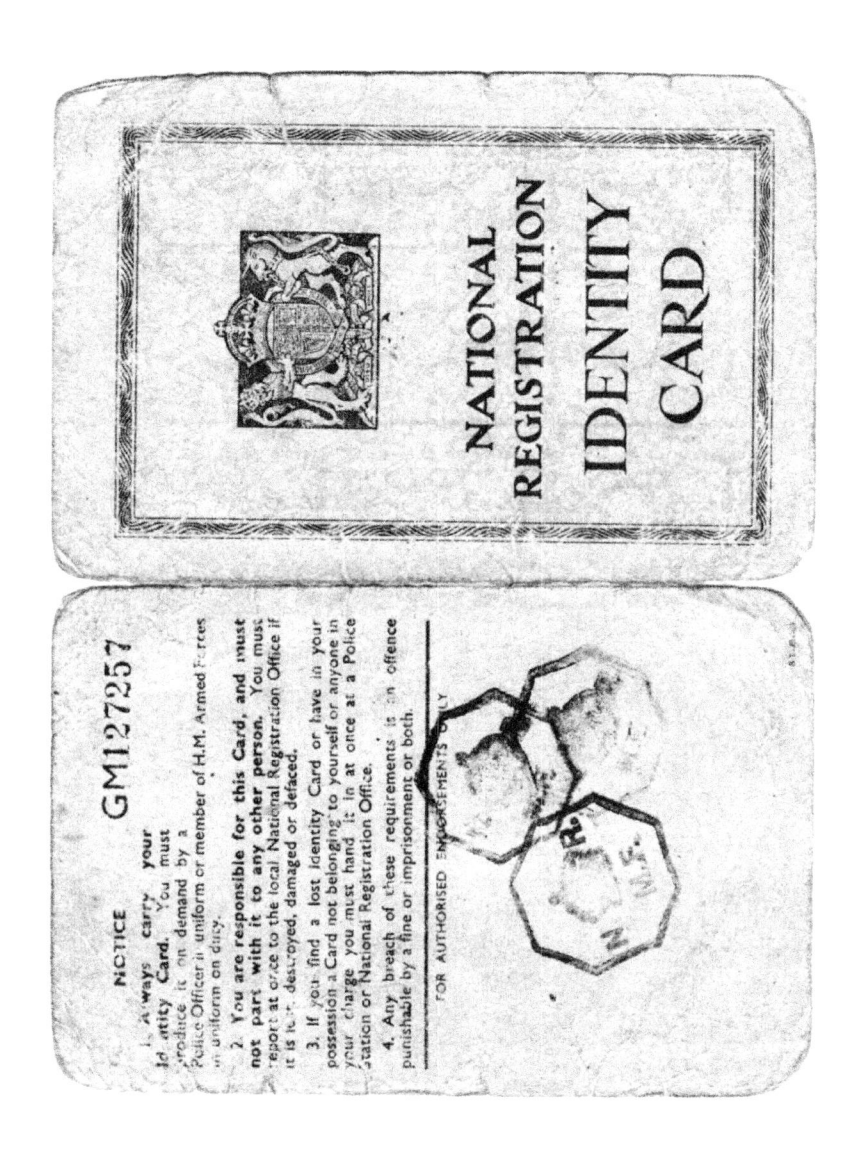

Jack Blane
National Identity Card
Issued 1946 for his demob from the army.

National Identity Card Inner
Move to Whitely Crescent 1948

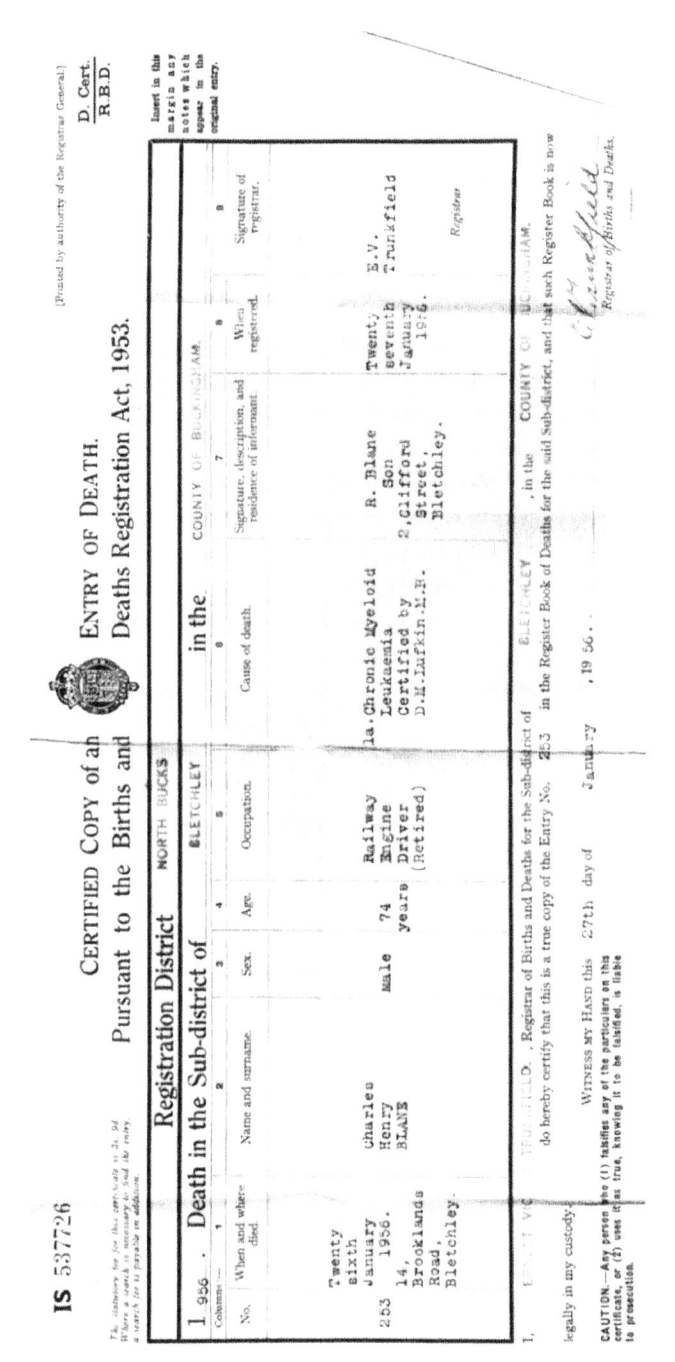

Jack Blane

CERTIFIED COPY of an ENTRY OF DEATH.
Pursuant to the Births and Deaths Registration Act, 1953.

IS 537726

Registration District **NORTH BUCKS**

Death in the Sub-district of **BLETCHLEY** in the COUNTY OF BUCKINGHAM.

No.	When and where died.	Name and surname.	Sex.	Age.	Occupation.	Cause of death.	Signature, description, and residence of informant.	When registered.	Signature of registrar.
253	Twenty sixth January 1956. 14, Brooklands Road, Bletchley.	Charles Henry BLANE	Male	74 years	Railway Engine Driver (Retired)	1a. Chronic Myeloid Leukaemia Certified by D.M.Lufkin.M.B.	R. Blane Son 2, Gifford Street, Bletchley.	Twenty seventh January 1956.	E.V. Trunkfield Registrar

I, ..., Registrar of Births and Deaths for the Sub-district of ELETCHLEY, in the COUNTY OF BUCKINGHAM, do hereby certify that this is a true copy of the Entry No. 253 in the Register Book of Deaths for the said Sub-district, and that such Register Book is now legally in my custody.

WITNESS MY HAND this 27th day of January, 19 56.

Charles Henry Blane Death Certificate 1956
His age at death would seem to confirm a birth year of 1881

Jean Blane Flannery

Death of Mr. C. H. Blane

Mr. Charles Henry Blane, of 14 Brooklands-road, Bletchley, died on Thursday, after six months illness. He was 74 years old.

Mr. Blane was a native of Haslingfield, Cambridgeshire, but came to Bletchley at the age of 16 years. He worked on the railway for nearly 50 years until he reached the retiring age of 65 and ended his career, being an engine driver when he retired.

He was a member of the N.U.R., of the local Labour Party, and of the Social Club.

Mr. and Mrs. Blane celebrated their golden wedding anniversary three years ago. They have lived in Brooklands-road for 43 years.

He leaves his widow, Mrs. M. Blane, and seven sons and one daughter, Mr. C. H. Blane, Mr. H. J. Blane, Felixstowe, Mr. D. F. Blane, Sandown, Mr. R. Blane, Mr. B. Blane, Mr. J. Blane, Mr. M. S. Blane, and Mrs. M. B. Osmond.

Charles Henry Blane local newspaper death notice

Jack Blane

CERTIFIED COPY of an ENTRY OF DEATH
Issued at a fee of 2/- in pursuance of and for the purposes of the First Schedule to the
INDUSTRIAL ASSURANCE AND FRIENDLY SOCIETIES ACT 1948

DEATH		Entry No. 69

Registration district
Sub-district
Administrative area

1. Date and place of death: **First, June, 1971** Renny Lodge Hospital, Newport Pagnell
2. Name and surname: **May Elizabeth Margaret Fraser Blane**
3. Sex: Female
4. Maiden surname of woman who has married: Powell
5. Date and place of birth: 15th. July, 1878 Rotherhithe, London
6. Occupation and usual address: Widow of Charles Blane, Railway Engine Driver. Renny Lodge Hospital, Newport Pagnell
7. (a) Name and surname of informant: Henry James Blane
   (b) Qualification: Son
   (c) Usual address: 45, Mount Pleasant, Aspley Guise, Bletchley
8. Cause of death: 1a. Bronchopneumonia Certified by G.F. Cockings, M.B.
9. I certify that the particulars given by me above are true to the best of my knowledge and belief — H.J. Blane — Signature of informant
10. Date of registration: Second, June, 1971
11. Signature of registrar: G.L. Trunkfield, Registrar.

Certified to be a true copy of an entry in a register in my custody.
Registrar — 4th. June, 1971 — Date

Person to whom issued: Name and surname (in full): Margaret Bessie Osmond
Address: The Bungalow, Caldecote, Bow Brickhill, Bletchley, Bucks.
Relationship to deceased: child (delete those inapplicable)
Note:—Child includes an adopted child.

EA 480015

CAUTION:- Any person who (1) falsifies any of the particulars on this certificate or (2) uses a falsified certificate as true, knowing it to be false, is liable to prosecution.

May Elizabeth Margaret Fraser Blane
Death Certificate 1971

Jack Blane Smallpox Vaccination Certificate 1973
There had been a small outbreak in London that Spring

LONDON BRICK COMPANY LIMITED
SOCIAL & SPORTS ASSOCIATION

MEMBERSHIP CARD
(NOT TRANSFERABLE)

Honorary Life Membership
(Retired Employee and Spouse)

SPECIAL NOTE

Production of this Card at any Works Social and Sports Association, Club or Ground entitles you to Honorary Membership of that Club, subject to the Rules and Bye-laws of the particular Social and Sports Association

---

The holder of this Card, whilst using the facilities provided, must comply with the Rules and Regulations as laid down by the Social and Sports Association.
THIS CARD MUST BE PRODUCED TO THE STEWARD, DOORKEEPER, OR OTHER OFFICERS WHEN REQUIRE

Serial No.   Name
1174   MR. JACK BLANE

Member's Usual Signature.
THIS CARD IS INVALID UNLESS SIGNED BY THE MEMBER

Issued by .... STEWARTBY .... Association

Jack Blane Honorary Life Membership Card for Stewartby Club as a retired employee
(actual colour of the card is what we called "Brick Company Red')

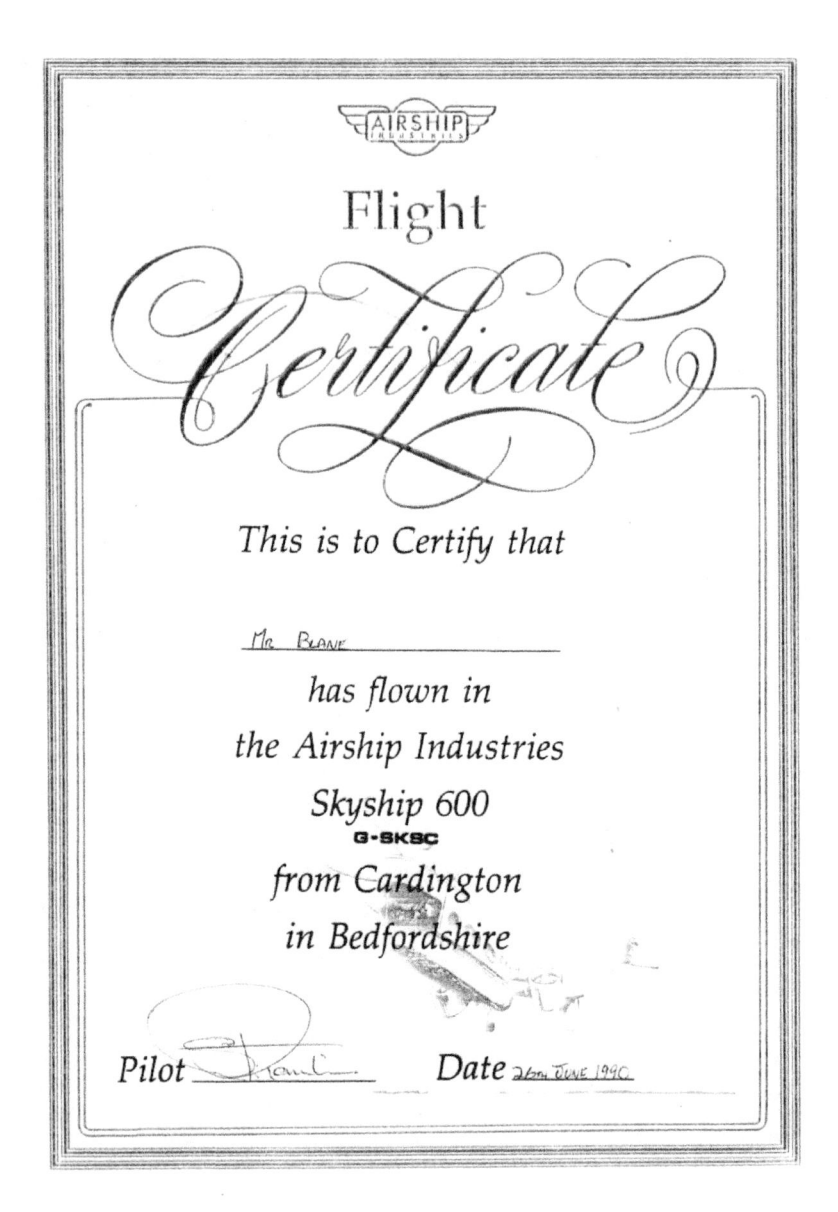

> **Flight Certificate**
>
> This is to Certify that
>
> _Mr Blane_
>
> has flown in
> the Airship Industries
> Skyship 600
> G-SKSC
> from Cardington
> in Bedfordshire
>
> Pilot _____ Date 26th June 1990

I couldn't resist adding this certificate from my parents first airship flight.

Jack Blane

CERTIFIED COPY OF AN ENTRY
Pursuant to the Births and Deaths Registration Act 1953

BAV 787544

DEATH

Entry No. 229

Registration district Bedford
Administrative area The Borough of Bedford
Sub-district Bedford

1. **Date and place of death**
Eighth December 2012
Salvete 15 Rothsay Place Bedford

2. **Name and surname**
Jack BLANE

3. **Sex**
Male

4. **Maiden surname of woman who has married**

5. **Date and place of birth**
Fourteenth August 1918
Bletchley Buckinghamshire

6. **Occupation and usual address**
Club Secretary-Sport and Social (retired)
Husband of Kitty BLANE Housewife (retired)
Salvete 15 Rothsay Place Bedford

7. (a) **Name and surname of informant**
Carole HULATT

(b) **Qualification**
Daughter
Present at the death

(c) **Usual address**
Flat 14 Russell Court Bushmead Avenue Bedford Bedfordshire

8. I certify that the particulars given by me above are true to the best of my knowledge and belief

C Hulatt — Signature of informant

9. **Cause of death**
I (a) Metastatic Prostate Cancer

II Frailty

Certified by D C Fenske MBBS

10. **Date of registration**
Thirteenth December 2012

11. **Signature of registrar**
S E Chandler
Deputy Registrar

Certified to be a true copy of an entry in a register in my custody.

S E Chandler { Deputy Registrar } Date 13-12-2012

System No. 507748204

CAUTION: THERE ARE OFFENCES RELATING TO FALSIFYING OR ALTERING A CERTIFICATE AND USING OR POSSESSING A FALSE CERTIFICATE. ©CROWN COPYRIGHT

WARNING: A CERTIFICATE IS NOT EVIDENCE OF IDENTITY.

Jack Blane Death Certificate
2012

FAMILY LINE

Blane

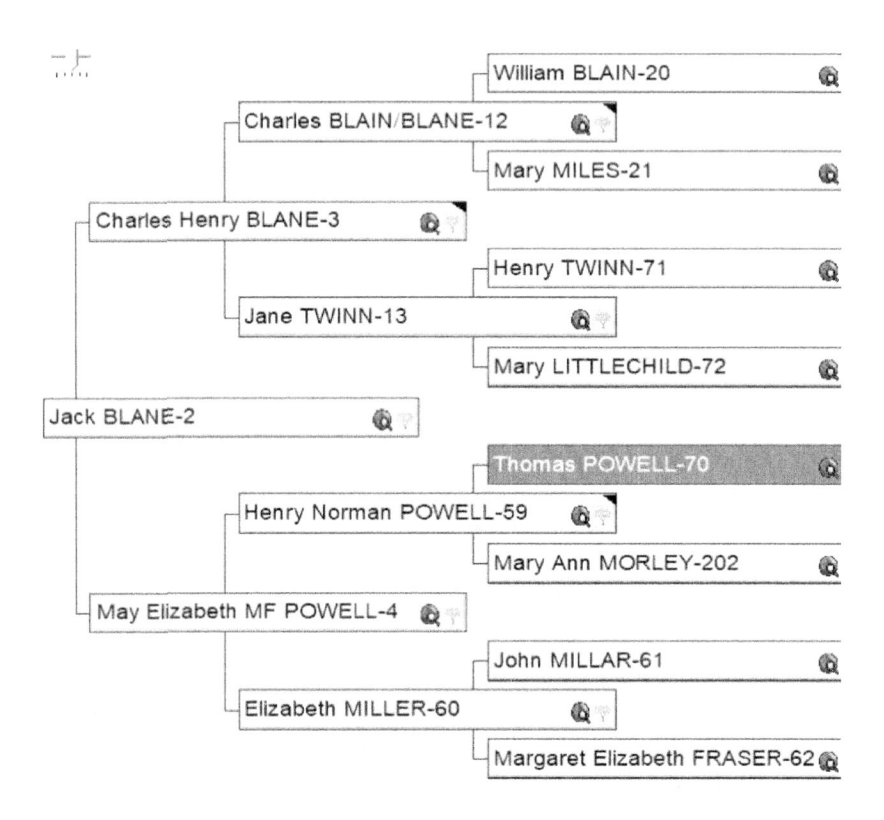

```
                                    ┌─ William BLAIN-20
                   ┌─ Charles BLAIN/BLANE-12
                   │                └─ Mary MILES-21
   ┌─ Charles Henry BLANE-3
   │               │                ┌─ Henry TWINN-71
   │               └─ Jane TWINN-13
   │                                └─ Mary LITTLECHILD-72
Jack BLANE-2
   │                                ┌─ Thomas POWELL-70
   │               ┌─ Henry Norman POWELL-59
   │               │                └─ Mary Ann MORLEY-202
   └─ May Elizabeth MF POWELL-4
                   │                ┌─ John MILLAR-61
                   └─ Elizabeth MILLER-60
                                    └─ Margaret Elizabeth FRASER-62
```

The numbers identify the person and in addition, denote the order in which each was added to the database.

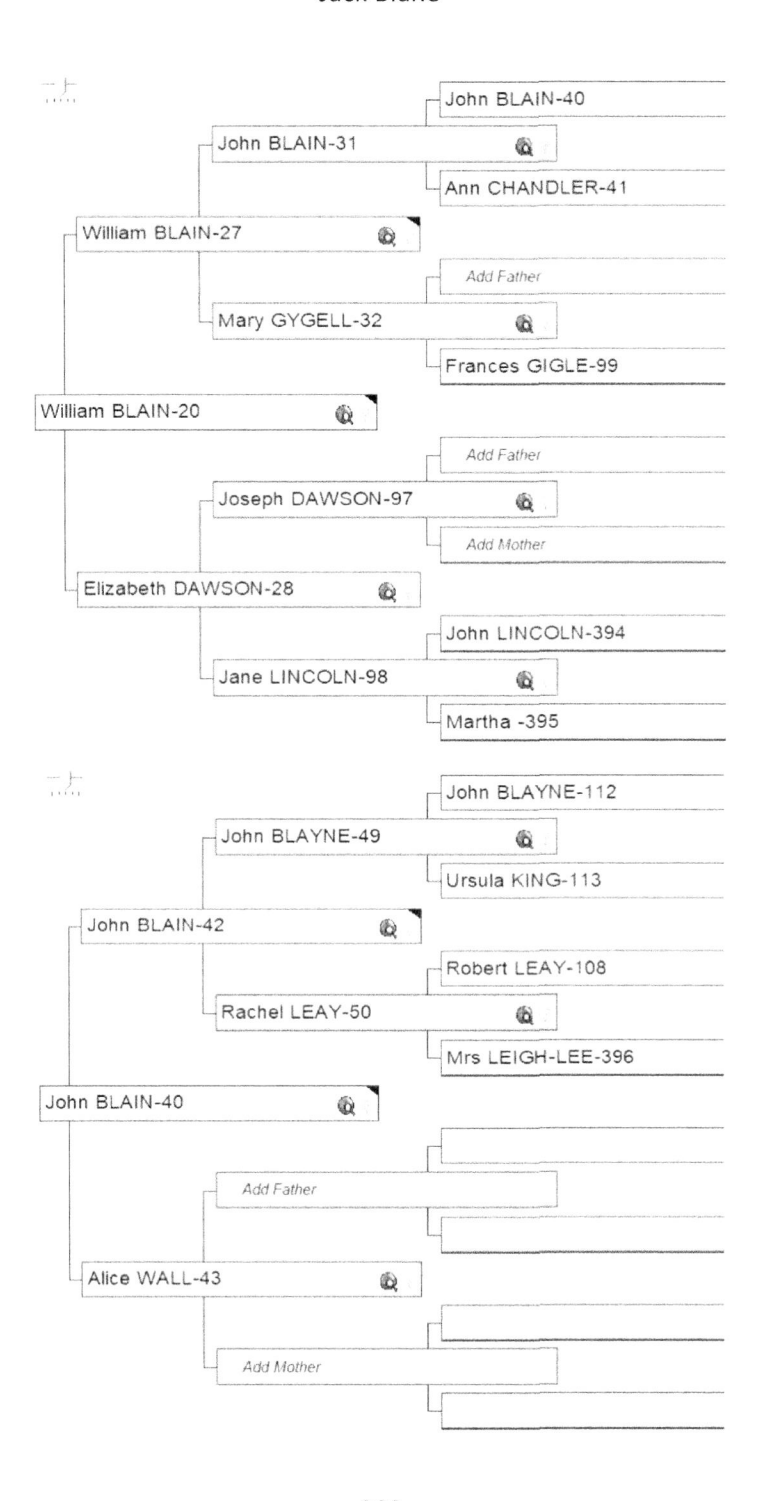

Jack Blane

- William BLAIN-20
  - William BLAIN-27
    - John BLAIN-31
      - John BLAIN-40
      - Ann CHANDLER-41
    - Mary GYGELL-32
      - Add Father
      - Frances GIGLE-99
  - Elizabeth DAWSON-28
    - Joseph DAWSON-97
      - Add Father
      - Add Mother
    - Jane LINCOLN-98
      - John LINCOLN-394
      - Martha -395

- John BLAIN-40
  - John BLAIN-42
    - John BLAYNE-49
      - John BLAYNE-112
      - Ursula KING-113
    - Rachel LEAY-50
      - Robert LEAY-108
      - Mrs LEIGH-LEE-396
  - Alice WALL-43
    - Add Father
    - Add Mother

209

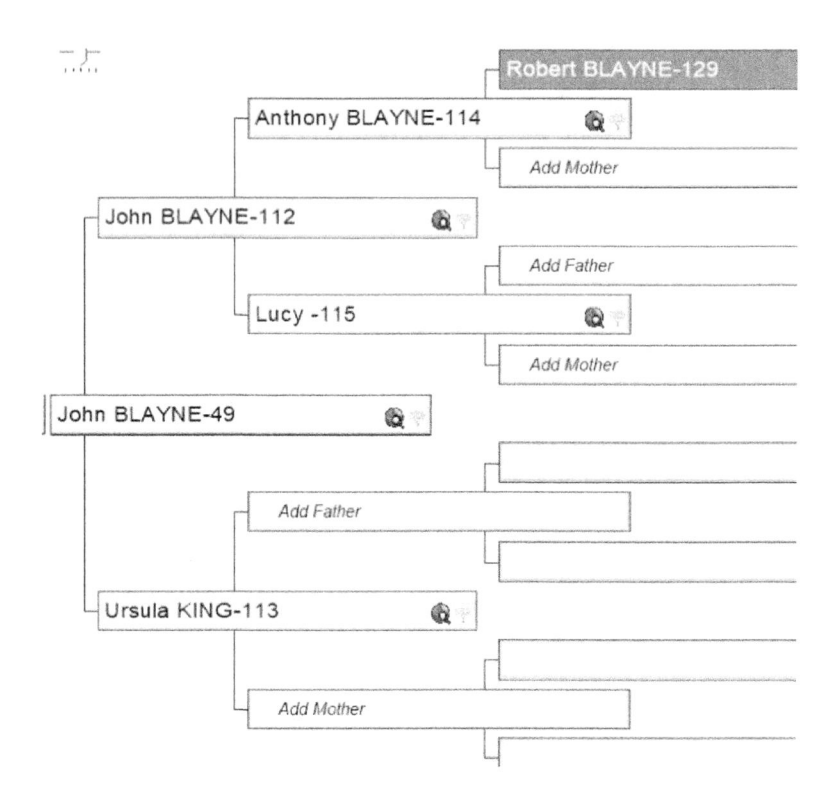

```
                                          ┌─ Robert BLAYNE-129
                      ┌─ Anthony BLAYNE-114 ─┤
                      │                      └─ Add Mother
      ┌─ John BLAYNE-112 ─┤
      │                   │                  ┌─ Add Father
      │                   └─ Lucy -115 ──────┤
      │                                      └─ Add Mother
John BLAYNE-49 ─┤
      │                   ┌─ Add Father
      │                   │
      └─ Ursula KING-113 ─┤
                          │
                          └─ Add Mother
```

That is as far back as records take us.

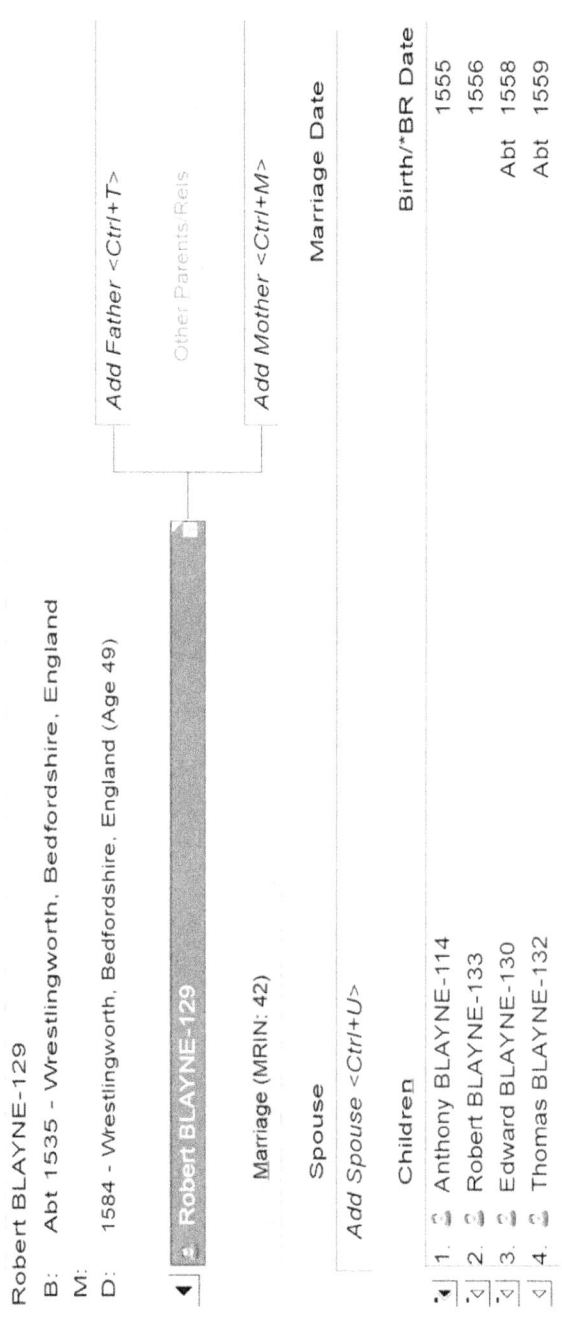

Robert BLAYNE-129
B: Abt 1535 - Wrestlingworth, Bedfordshire, England
M:
D: 1584 - Wrestlingworth, Bedfordshire, England (Age 49)

Robert BLAYNE-129

Marriage (MRIN: 42)

Spouse

Add Spouse <Ctrl+U>

Children	Birth/*BR Date
1. Anthony BLAYNE-114	1555
2. Robert BLAYNE-133	1556
3. Edward BLAYNE-130	Abt 1558
4. Thomas BLAYNE-132	Abt 1559

Add Father <Ctrl+T>

Other Parents Rels

Add Mother <Ctrl+M>

Marriage Date

The earliest Blane/Blayne record we have.

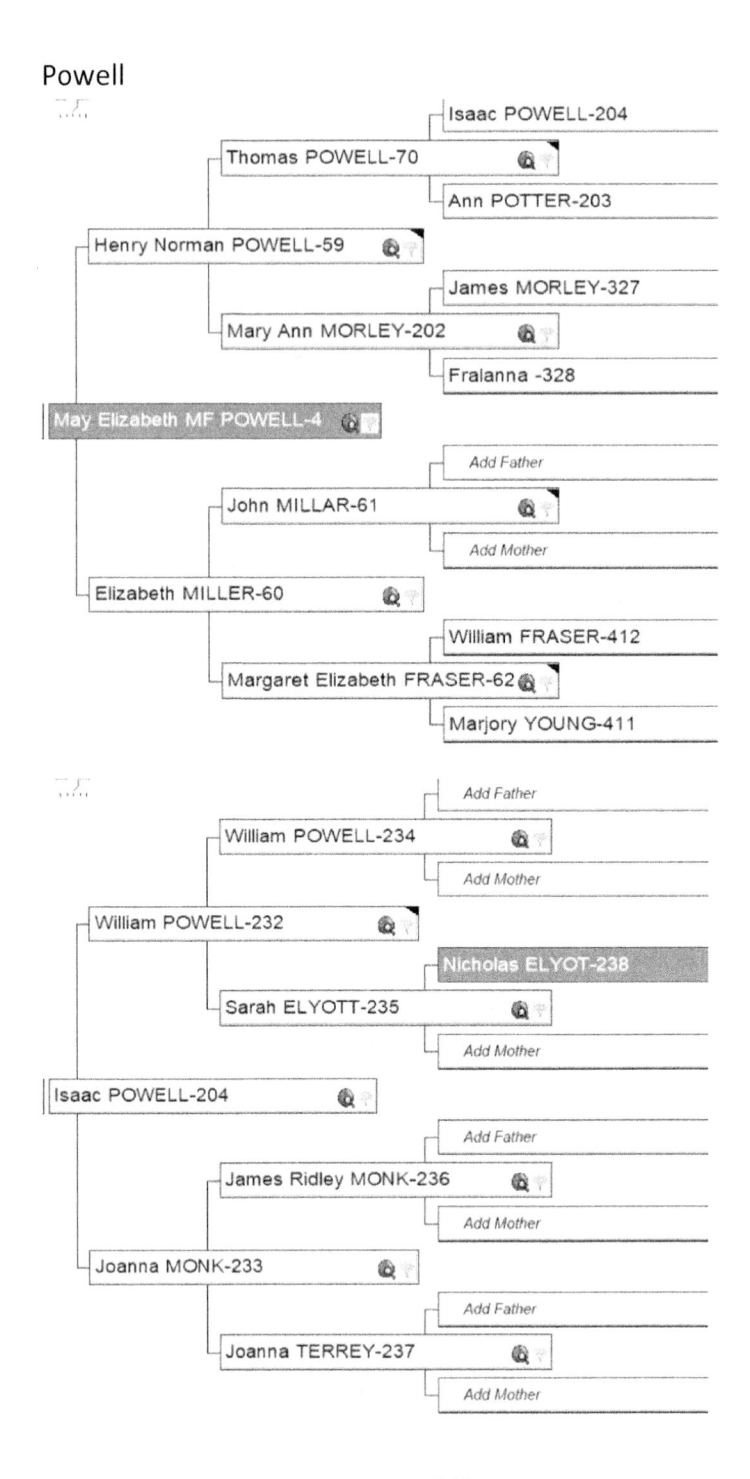

Powell

- Henry Norman POWELL-59
  - Thomas POWELL-70
    - Isaac POWELL-204
    - Ann POTTER-203
  - Mary Ann MORLEY-202
    - James MORLEY-327
    - Fralanna -328

- May Elizabeth MF POWELL-4

- Elizabeth MILLER-60
  - John MILLAR-61
    - Add Father
    - Add Mother
  - Margaret Elizabeth FRASER-62
    - William FRASER-412
    - Marjory YOUNG-411

- Isaac POWELL-204
  - William POWELL-232
    - William POWELL-234
      - Add Father
      - Add Mother
    - Sarah ELYOTT-235
      - Nicholas ELYOT-238
      - Add Mother
  - Joanna MONK-233
    - James Ridley MONK-236
      - Add Father
      - Add Mother
    - Joanna TERREY-237
      - Add Father
      - Add Mother

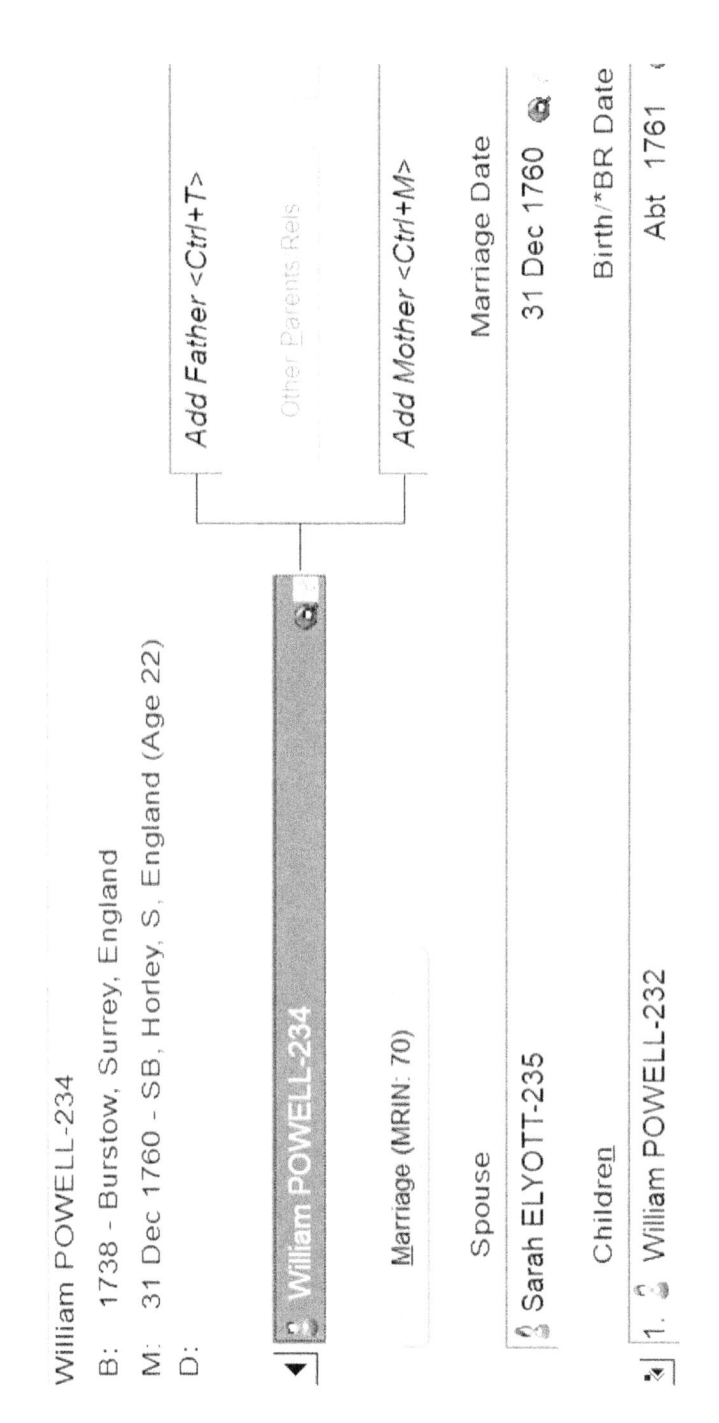

William POWELL-234
B: 1738 - Burstow, Surrey, England
M: 31 Dec 1760 - SB, Horley, S, England (Age 22)
D:

William POWELL-234

Marriage (MRIN: 70)

Spouse
Sarah ELYOTT-235

Children
1. William POWELL-232

Add Father <Ctrl+T>
Other Parents Rels
Add Mother <Ctrl+M>

Marriage Date
31 Dec 1760

Birth/*BR Date
Abt 1761

The earliest Powell record we have.

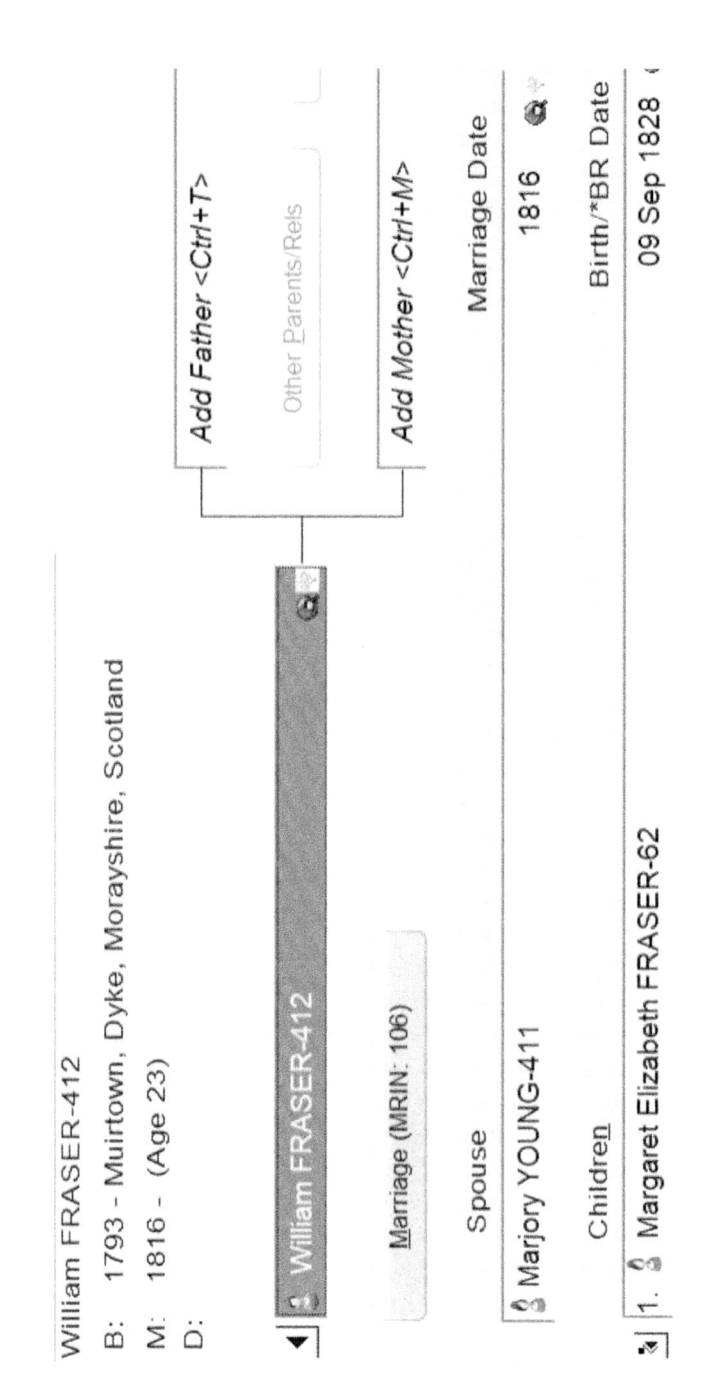

William FRASER-412
B: 1793 - Muirtown, Dyke, Morayshire, Scotland
M: 1816 - (Age 23)
D:

William FRASER-412

Marriage (MRIN: 106)

Spouse
Marjory YOUNG-411

Children
1. Margaret Elizabeth FRASER-62

Add Father <Ctrl+T>
Other Parents/Rels
Add Mother <Ctrl+M>

Marriage Date
1816

Birth/*BR Date
09 Sep 1828

The earliest Fraser record we have

WHAT'S IN A NAME?
All in the Family

The idea for this chapter grew after I began to think about my paternal grandmother's four given names and why they had been chosen for her. May Elizabeth Margaret Fraser is quite a mouthful for a young child.

I realised that she had been named for her maternal ancestry, as far back as we have records. May was the diminutive of her great grandmother Marjory. Elizabeth was her mother's name, Margaret that of her grandmother. Fraser was the family name of the maternal line.

From there, it didn't take me long to become curious about the meaning and origin of the surnames in my father's family tree.

So here they are, in alphabetical order.

BLAYNE AND ITS VARIANTS

The name Blayne dates back to the Boernicians. These were a mix of Scottish Picts, Angles and Vikings, one of the ancient clans of the Scottish-English borderlands. They are considered to be the ancient founding peoples of the north.

The surname Blayne itself was first found in Ayrshire. The Blaynes held a family seat there from very ancient times, possibly long before the arrival of William the Conqueror in 1066.

Various origins are listed for the name. One is that it comes from the Gaelic bleen, yellow. Another possible meaning is lean.

There was also an early Celtic saint of that name.

Variations of the name came about as mediaeval scribes spelled names phonetically rather than by any over-arching set of rules. So we have Blain, Blane, Blaine, and Blayns.

CHANDLER

Chandler, with its variant spellings, originated in Anglo-Saxon mediaeval England. It derives from the Old English chaundeler and chandeler, which come from the Old French word chandelier.

This in turn is derived from the Latin candelarius, which itself comes from candela, meaning candle. That derives from candere, meaning to be bright. So the name has been through quite a transformation.

Chandler was used as a surname when a family member worked making and selling candles. More rarely, it may also have been given to someone who had the responsibility of lighting the candles in a large house, or one who paid rent in the form of wax or candles.

DAWSON

Dawson as a name came to England in the 11th century wave of migration set off by the Norman Conquest. The family was originally from Osonvilla, near Dieppe in Normandy. It is from here that the name D'Oson, from Oson, came into use. In time it became anglicised to Dawson.

The surname is first found in England in the West Riding of Yorkshire at North Bierely, a township in the parish of Bradford: Wapentake of Morley.

ELYOTT

I have found more than one explanation of the origin of this name. And it seems to have originated in various parts of England at around the same time.

One source considers its origin to be in the Hebrew Elias or Elijah, meaning The Lord is my God.

Then we have original Anglo-Saxon surnames from Northumbria, including Aelwold, Ellwald, Elaund, Elwods and Elyars, which all seem to have eventually mixed together.

There are records in the Domesday Book of the name spelled as Ailiet, thought to originate from an Old English name meaning noble gate.

The name Eliot has a Breton origin. The West Country Eliots may have been among those Bretons accompanying William the Conqueror, who were originally rewarded with lands in Devon. And in the late 12th century holders of the name were also to be found in South East England.

Last but not least, there is the Scottish clan Elliot.

Given that those transcribing names frequently used whatever spelling they felt right phonetically, any of the above are possibilities for "our" Elyott.

FRASER/FRAZER

It is thought that the Frasers may have originally come from Anjou, in France. The name could be an altered form of the French Fresel, which meant ribbon or braid in Old French. It was probably the nickname for the sellers of such goods.

However, the surnames Fresel and Frezel were historically centred on Upper Normandy and Artois/French Flanders, not Anjou.

The name sounds like a derived form of fraise, French for strawberry, and such popular phonetic renderings explain many badges and coats of arms.

The first Fraser to appear in the records was in Scotland, at about 1160, when Simon Fraser held lands at Keith in East Lothian.

GYGELL/GIGLE

Gygell/Gigle and Giggle are variants on an Anglo-Saxon surname. This came from the forename Jukel (or Gikel), referring to the son of Jukel.

The names Juhel and Gicquel derive from the ancient Breton name, Judicaël. These names became Jukel or Gikel in mediaeval English.

The Latin forms of the names were first found in the Domesday Book. Gykell, Jukel de Jertheburc, was listed in Lincolnshire records c1170 - around a century later.

JENNINGS

Jennings is of early mediaeval English origin, although it later became associated with both Wales and Ireland.

Recorded in the spellings of Jennings, Jennins and Jennens, it refers to son of Janyn or Jenyn, a diminutive of the name John and meaning Little John. Its use as a surname dates back to the late 13th century.

John itself derives from the Hebrew name Yochanan, meaning Jehovah has favoured (me with a son).

The name John was introduced into England by the crusaders in the 12th century.

KING

King dates back to Anglo-Saxon times and comes from the Old English cyning, originally meaning tribal leader.

This was commonly given as a nickname to a man who carried himself like royalty, or who played the part of the king in a mediaeval pageant.

It might also be used by a man who served in a royal household.

The surname is first found recorded in Devon, around 1050.

LEAHY

Leahy is an Irish name, the original Gaelic form of O Laochdha being derived from the word laochdha, meaning heroic.

The surname was first recorded in County Tipperary, where the Leahys held a family seat from ancient times, as descendants of the tribe of Uaithne.

LEIGH-LEE

This could simply be a variant of Leahy, written as the transcriber heard it.

Lee may be a modern form of the ancient Irish name O'Laithain. Leigh is sometimes used as an alternative to Lee but can also mean a meadow or glade in Old English.

LINCOLN

The movement of people following the Norman Conquest brought the Lincoln family name to the British Isles. The name is taken from the city of Lincoln in Lincolnshire.

The placename itself may be derived from the British name Lindo, which means lake, and the Latin word colonia, which means settlement or colony.

Alternatively, the name may derive from Lin in the Gaelic, Welsh, and Cornish-British, signifying a pool, pond, or lake, and coln, the ridge or neck of a hill, so called from its situation.

The original city occupied the top and side of a steep hill on the river Witham.

Unsurprisingly, the surname Lincoln was first found in Lincolnshire - in 1086.

LITTLECHILD

The surname Littlechild was most likely used as a Saxon nickname for somebody tall or large, as in Robin Hood's Little John. It can first be found in records of the 13th century. The Littlechilds held a family seat in Essex as Lords of the Manor.

Although the language of the courts remained French for three centuries after the Norman Conquest, and Norman practices prevailed, this is another Saxon surname that survived.

MILES

The name was introduced to England by the Normans via Old French, from the Germanic personal name Milo, the origin of which is unknown.

In English documents of the Middle Ages the name can be found written in what was also the Latinised form Milo, although the normal Middle English form was Mile. So the final s would represent the possessive ending, ie son or servant of Mile.

It also originated as the occupational name for a servant or retainer, from the Latin miles, soldier.

The surname is first found in Lincolnshire, where a Johannes filius Mile was listed 1150-1160.

MILLAR/MILLER

This is a simple one. Millar is the Old English version of Miller, one who works in a mill, specifically grinding grain into flour. The meaning of the word hasn't changed with the centuries.

MONK

Anglo-Scottish, this surname derives from the pre-7th century word munuc, from the Middle English munk or monk. In Old English it was munuc or munec from the Latin monachus. This in its turn comes from the Greek monakhos, solitary.

It was originally a nickname for someone of monkish habits or appearance, or an occupational name for a servant employed at a monastery. Later the name assumed the religious meaning with which it became associated.

As a surname, Monk was first recorded in Devon.

MORLEY

This is another quite simple one. The Morley name is derived from any of several places so named. There are Morleys in Cheshire, in Derbyshire, County Durham, Norfolk, and West Yorkshire, and a Moreleigh in Devon.

The place names come from the Old English words mor, meaning marsh, and leah, meaning a clearing in the woods. So there is a connection in the name to Leigh.

The surname Morley was first found in Derbyshire at Morley, a parish in the union of Belper, apparently sometime in the 13th century. And some 600 years later our Millar forebears were found living there.

POWELL

Powell is an English surname of Welsh origin. It is a patronymic form of the Welsh name Hywel (which became anglicized as Howell), with the prefix ap meaning "son of." Together they form ap Hywel, or son of Hywel, and eventually Powell.

The general consensus is that Hywell means eminent or possibly conspicuous. It may refer to Saint Hywell, a 6th century disciple of Saint Teilo.

ROWLEY

Rowley is another surname thought to have derived from various places of the same name, in this instance in Devon, County Durham, Staffordshire, and Yorkshire. They are so named from the Old English, pre-7th century ruh: rough, overgrown, and leah as with Morley. So we have a rough or overgrown clearing.

However, the name could have been Norman in origin too. Roulat is now rather rare in France. But Roulet (and Roullet) and Roulot are fairly common.

The surname Rowley was first found recorded in Cheshire, where the family claimed to be of Saxon blood.

TERREY

The name comes from the Norman personal name Therry. This in turn comes from the Germanic Theodoric, meaning ruler of the people. The Old English form of the name was Theodric and Terry became the diminutive in mediaeval times.

Edward the Confessor (c1004-1066) employed a German goldsmith named Theoderic for some of his coinage design. So it is likely that the name in Britain predates the coming of the Normans

The surname Terrey was first recorded in Kent, in the early 12th century.

TWINN

The name is a variant of Twin, nickname surname for one of a pair of twins. It derives from the Old English pre-7th Century (ge)twinn, meaning twofold, double, a derivation of twa, two, or the Middle English twin, with the same meaning

The surname was first referenced in Hampshire, in the 13th century, the family being Lords of a Manor.

WALL

Simple and obvious, the surname Wall originally referred to a person who lived beside a stone wall. This might be a wall used to fortify a castle or city, or a sea wall.

Members of the Wall family are known to have been established in Gloucestershire prior to the Norman Conquest.

WRIGHT

The surname Wright is another dating back to the ancient Boernicians of the Scottish-English border region. It is a derivative of the Old English word wryhta (or wyrhta), from around 700 AD. Its meaning was a worker or shaper of wood. Later it became used as an occupational description. For example, we have shipwright and wheelwright.

The earliest record of the name is in Berwickshire.

YOUNG

The surname Young has a history dating back to the Anglo-Saxon tribes of Britain. Meaning one who is very young, from the Old English words yong and yung, it was a descriptive name used to denote the younger of two bearers of the same personal name. This could be a son from his father or the younger of two relatives with the same name.

The name appears in the Anglo-Saxon Chronicle of 744 AD as Wilfer seo lunga. In 1296 a Walter Yonge is listed in the Subsidy Rolls for Sussex.

MAPS

Jean Blane Flannery

Approximate Locations of Family Homes

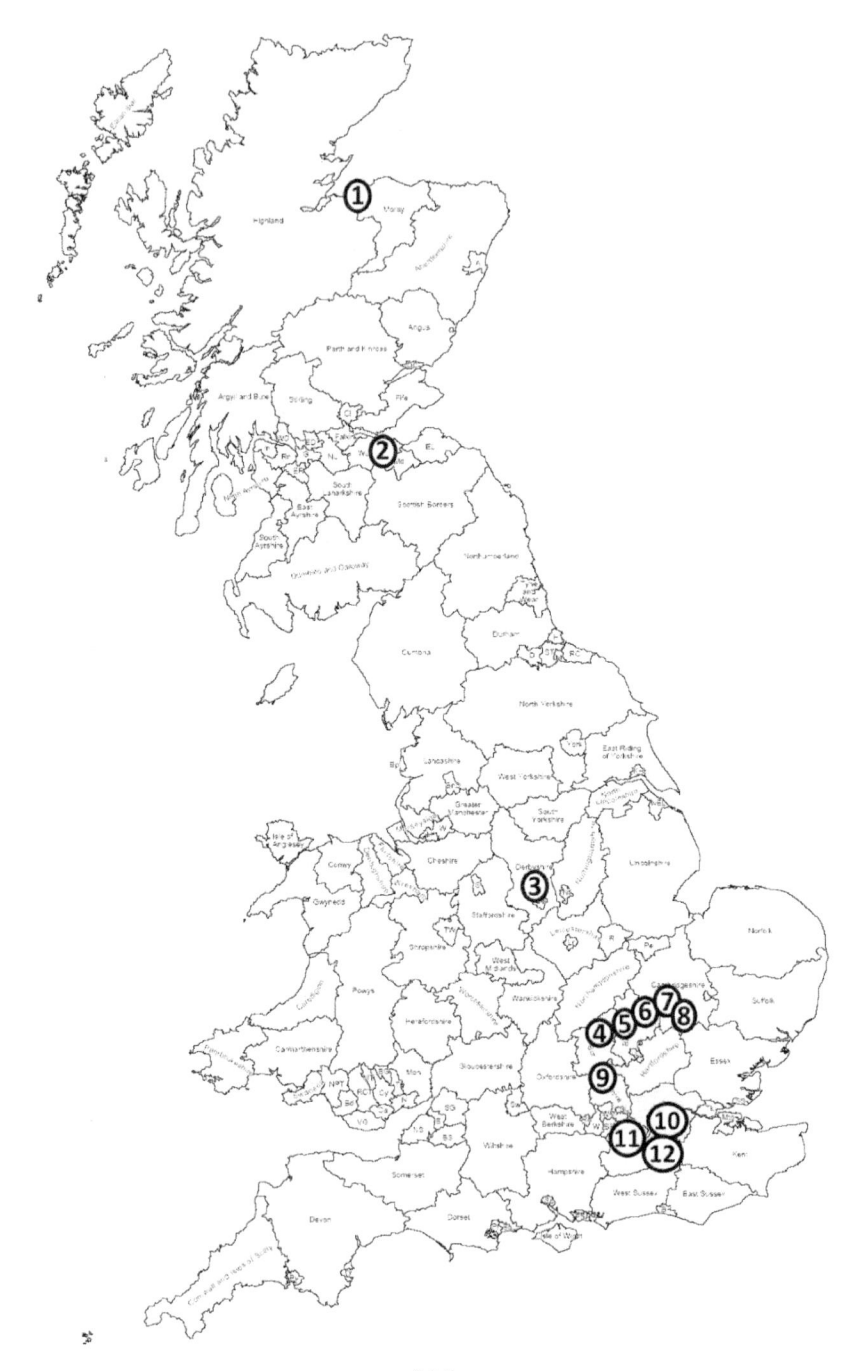

Key

1	Dyke area	Fraser
2	Edinburgh	Millar
3	Belper	Millar
4	Bletchley	Blane
5	Stewartby	Blane
6	Sandy Area	Blane
7	Haslingfield	Blane
	Barton	Blane
8	Duxford	Twinn/Blain
9	Aylesbury	Millar/Blane
10	Rotherhithe	Millar
11	Surrey	
	Woking	Millar
	Burstow	Powell
12	Horley	Powell

Aylesbury c1900

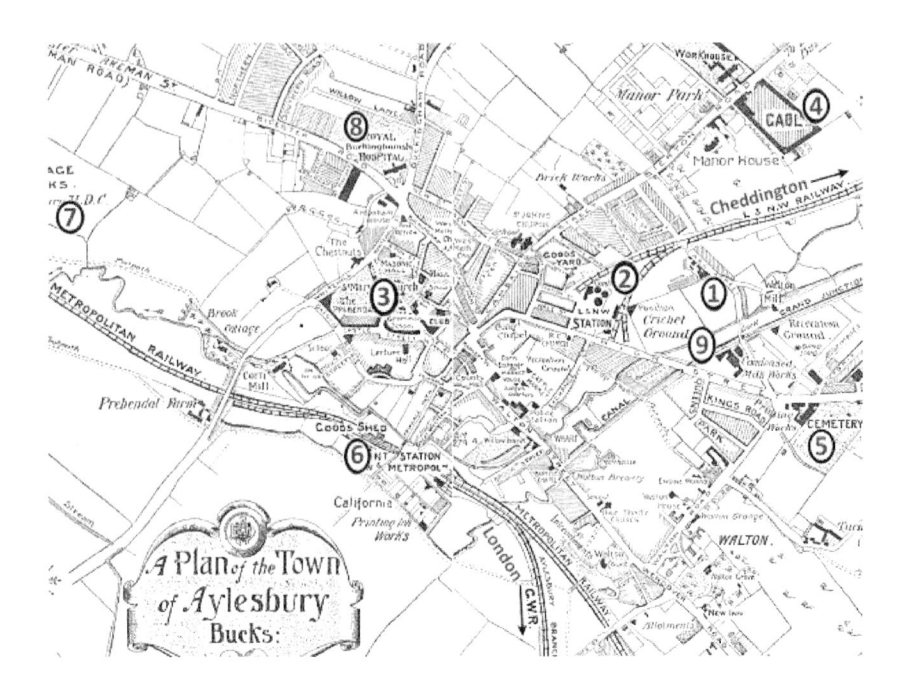

Key:

	1	Park Street
	2	Aylesbury - Cheddington L&BR Station
	3	St Mary's Church
	4	Women's Prison
	5	Cemetery
	6	Mainline Station for Great Western Railway
	7	Sewage Works
	8	Hospital (Infirmary)
	9	Grand Junction Canal Branch

Bletchley/Bedford Area

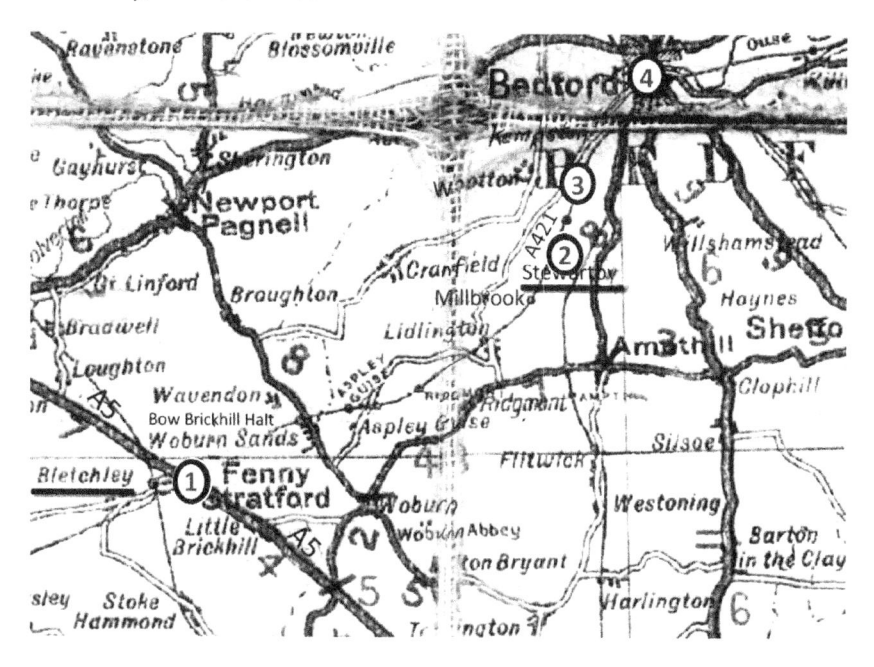

An old map of the area where my father lived all his life. You can see the roads, and the local railway line, quite clearly. With Fenny Stratford, rather than Bletchley, shown as the larger town, the map is certainly pre-WWII.

Cow Bridge Halt had been closed before we moved to Stewartby.

Key:

1   Bletchley/Fenny Stratford
2   Stewartby
3   Cow Bridge Halt, the stop for Elstow.
4   Bedford

The large figures show the distance between the road junctions in miles.

Railway Terrace area of Bletchley, behind the station carriage sheds.

Upper left is the railway bridge; once under that you are in Bletchley town itself.

Bletchley

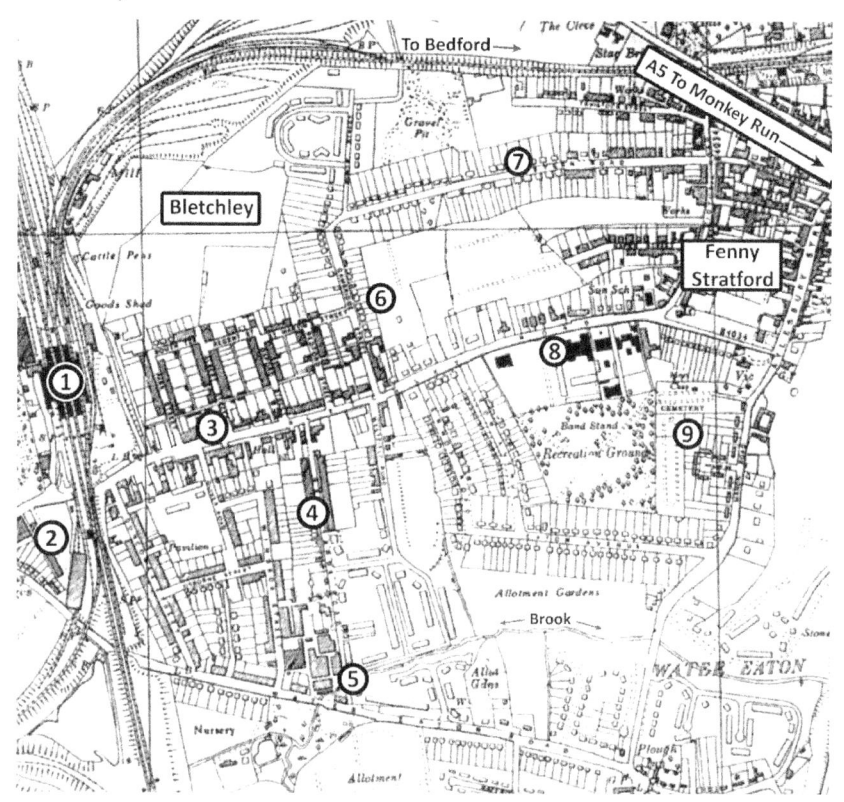

Key:

1 Railway Station
2 Railway Terrace
3 Cattle Market
4 Co-op
5 14 Brooklands Road, Jack's home until marriage in 1940
6 Brook where Martin went in
7 Cambridge Street, home from 1940 - 1948
8 Western Road, home from 1952-1954
9 Bletchley Road School
10 Cemetery where Margaret Millar interred

Jean Blane Flannery

Far Bletchley

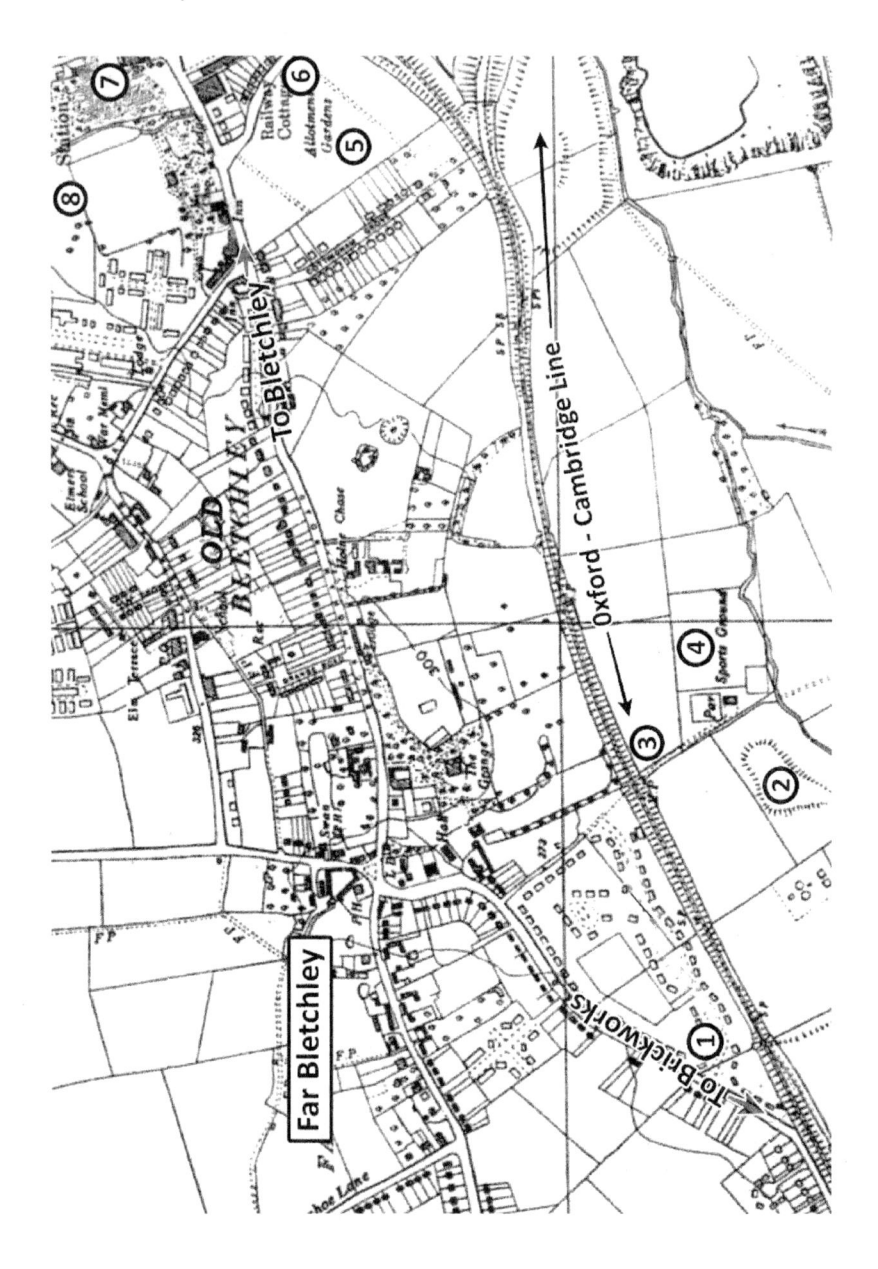

Key:

1   Number 1 Whiteley Crescent
     A brand new council house, home from 1948-1952
2   Knothole
3   Footpath
4   Sportsground
5   Allotments
6   Railway Terrace
7   Railway Station
8   Bletchley Park

Stewartby

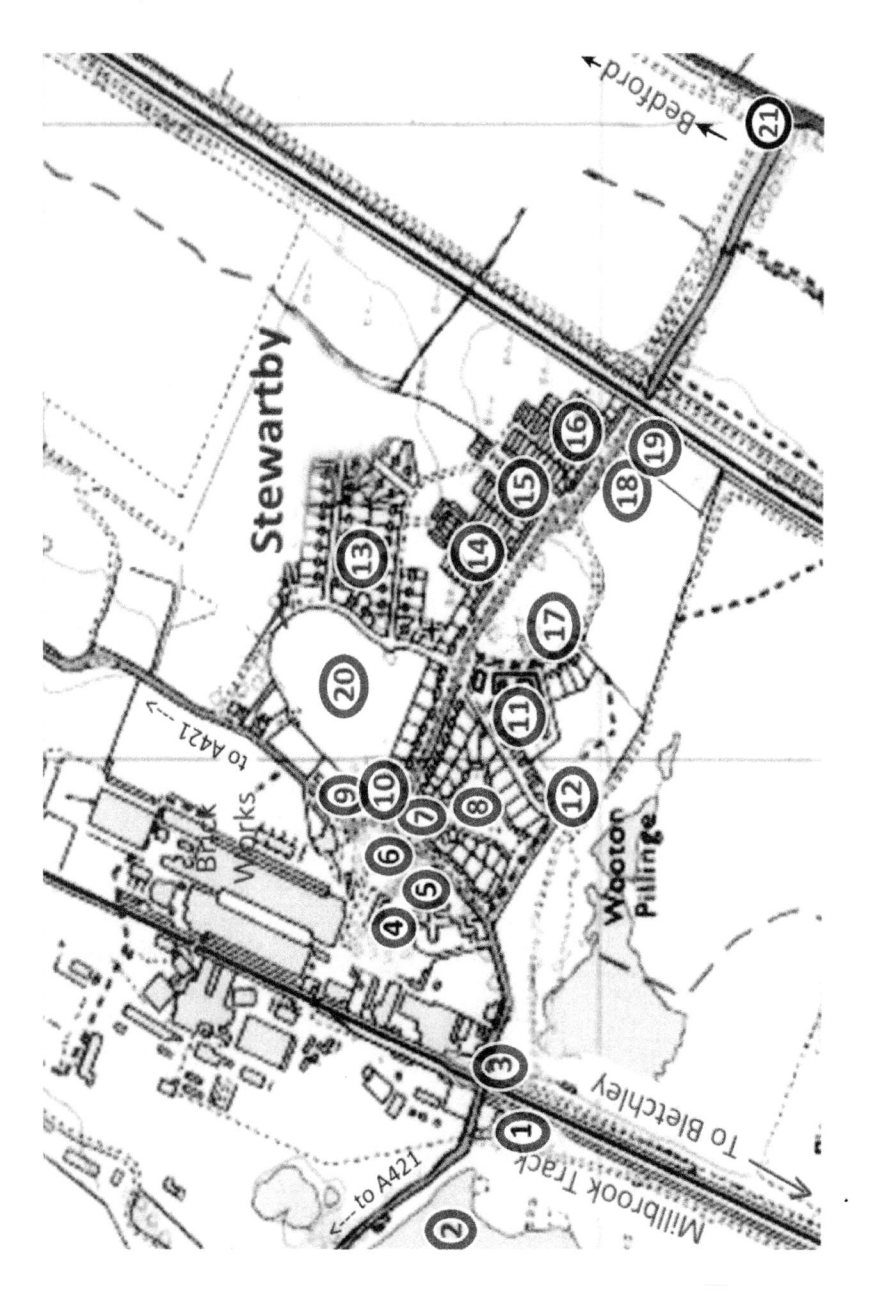

Key:

1. Knothole
2. Old Works Pond
3. Stewartby Halt
4. Swimming Pool
5. Laboratory
6. Bus Stop
7. Village Hall
8. Churchill Close
9. Stewartby Club
10. Co-op/Post Office
11. Schools
12. Old School Sports Field
13. "New Houses"
14. Alexander Close
15. Montgomery Close
16. Wavell Close, home from 1954-1998
17. Sir Malcolm Stewart Homes, The Crescent Home from 1998-2010
18. Carter's Farm
19. Allotments
20. Playing Field
21. Stewartby Turn

AYLESBURY

Aylesbury began as a Saxon settlement called Aegel's burgh. Burgh was a Saxon word meaning fort or fortified settlement. By the 11th century, Aylesbury had a mint and probably had a weekly market.

For centuries Aylesbury remained a large village rather than a town. Most of the people in Aylesbury made their living from farming rather than from industry. Mediaeval Aylesbury though was an administrative centre. Because of its weekly market, it served as a focal point for the surrounding villages.

From the 13th century, Aylesbury also had two fairs. In the Middle Ages fairs were like large markets. They were held annually, over the space of a few days. People came to the Aylesbury Fairs from all over Buckinghamshire.

In the 17th and 18th centuries there was a lace-making industry in Aylesbury. But it was the only significant industry in the town. There were some craftsmen such as carpenters, butchers, bakers, and blacksmiths, serving the local community, but that is all.

Aylesbury was also a coaching town. It was on several important routes and many stagecoaches stopped at the town's inns. Alfred the Great made Buckingham the county town of Buckinghamshire in 888. Then in the 18th century, Aylesbury became famous for the local breed of duck.

An infirmary opened in 1833. The first police force was formed in 1837. A cemetery opened in 1857. In the 1860s, a network of sewers was built and in 1867 a waterworks opened to supply the town. The coming of the railways began to change things.

The family lived on Park Street, close to the Aylesbury-Cheddington railway station.

Elizabeth Powell is shown as Assistant Warden at Woking Women's Prison in the 1881 and 1891 censuses. Her marital status is given as "widowed," I presume because a married woman would not have been employed. When Elizabeth moved to Aylesbury it was as Matron (Warden). The prison provided employment for quite a number of people.

We know that Aylesbury Gaol became the first female convict prison in England in 1895/96. This is how it looked in around 1900.

The inmates were brought here from all over England. And some had come originally from places such as Jersey, Ireland, and even France.

Mainly working-class women, they were used to undertaking hard jobs with long hours. They worked in the prison infirmary, kitchens, bakehouse, laundry and sewing-room.

LIFE IN A WOMEN'S PRISON
Female Convicts at Work in Aylesbury Gaol.

IN THE INFIRMARY

THE TAILORS' SHOP, WHERE ONLY MEN ARE EMPLOYED

IN THE KITCHEN

THE PRINCIPAL COOK

IN THE BAKEHOUSE

THE SEWING-ROOM

AT WORK IN THE LAUNDRY

But at this time, even though classed as a female prison, it was still only male prisoners who worked in the tailors' shop.

The railway was another area of employment. The Cheddington to Aylesbury railway line was an early branch line. Opening in 1839, local people formed the Aylesbury Railway to construct it.

It made a junction with the London and Birmingham Railway at Cheddington, which was also on the main line to Bletchley.

A little train known as the Cheddington Flyer chuntered back and forth along the seven mile track of the branch line. Never turning round, the train went frontwards and returned backwards.

Cheddington Flyer

When the L&BR merged with others in 1846 to form the London and North Western Railway, the line was in effect the Aylesbury branch of the LNWR.

The original Aylesbury-Cheddington line station, about three minutes' walk from the family home.

There was a railway crossing, seen here, half way along Park Street itself.

At the other end of the street ran a short, narrow branch (terminating in Aylesbury), of the Grand Junction Canal, later renamed the Grand Union.

Marston Gate Crossing and station looking in the Aylesbury direction, from which the signal suggests a train is arriving. On the right is a small weighbridge office and lamp hut. The ticket office with block instruments was in the timber building adjoining the house. The sign on the end of the timber building is of the LNWR period whilst the signals are tubular steel British Railways upper quadrant. The date is 24th January 1953.

Marston Gate Station, sadly derelict, on the Aylesbury-Cheddington line. Charles Henry would have known the station and crossing well.

Probably the last man to hold the post of Stationmaster at Marston Gate – Joseph Millar on the platform at Marston Gate. Note the timber platform on the 'up' side behind him that was used to stack milk churns.

We have no records of a Joseph Millar but it's possible that he was related. He would have lived in the brick house adjoining the station ticket office.

BLETCHLEY

Ken Barrow took this view, looking east towards Bletchley Road, from the railway bridge. The London Brick Company's AEC Mercury, passing the Park Hotel, dates the photograph to around 1958. The row of tin shops visible just past the railings on the left were very popular and included Mr Hurst's bicycle shop, Elizabeth's hat shop and the finest fish and chip shop in town.

Dad would recognise this view from his younger days, the buildings unchanged for decades. The Co-op butcher, managed by my Uncle Reg, stood just beyond the Park Hotel. The Co-op department store is the white building rear left.

Here is the butcher shop, decorated for Christmas sometime in the 1930's. Reg is second from left.

The original Bletchley was the area that became known later as Old Bletchley and Far Bletchley.

Whitely Crescent was in Far Bletchley and my first school was in Old Bletchley

The town's name, meaning Blæcca's clearing, is Anglo-Saxon. It was first recorded in the 12th century as Bicchelai, then in the 13th Century as Blechelegh, and from the 14th to the 16th century as Blecheley.

The area that we know simply as Bletchley was first known as Central Bletchley, to distinguish it from the older town area.

Just to the south of Fenny Stratford was the Romano-British town, Magiovinium, lying on both sides of the Roman road, the Watling Street. The modern name for the road is the A5.

The town as my father knew it, and I came to know it, had developed with the coming of the railway and as Bletchley became an important junction on the London Euston line.

Bletchley Station

Turning left out of the station approach leads into Bletchley itself. Coming under the railway bridge, on the right across Bletchley Road, was an apron of hard standing behind the footpath.

Fronting the hard standing stood The Park Hotel seen in the photo, the Co-op butcher's shop, a pub and the working men's club where Uncle Reg played billiards one evening a week. There was also a very nice fish and chip shop a bit further along.

On the left hand, station, side of the road the first buildings were a short row of funny little old corrugated iron roofed shops, known to all as the "tin shops."

Quite soon after passing those, on this side of the road and later the other, the pavement widened to become a very spacious area.

Tin Shops

The largest shop in Bletchley, a little further along into the town and still on the left, was the Co-op department store. There were a great many small, independent shops in both Bletchley and Fenny Stratford but very few that were part of a chain. And there was certainly only the one real department store.

Bletchley Road, Co-op in foreground

In 1911 Bletchley became the name of the Urban District that included Fenny Stratford. The population of the combined parishes was 5,166 in that year, as they began to merge.

By 1921 the combined population was still only around 5,500. In 1951, following the end of WWII, its population had grown to 10,919.

Throughout my father's childhood and right up until we moved to Stewartby, Bletchley remained a very pleasant, small market town.

The cattle market site held animal sales on one day a week and a general market on another. Each summer a funfair also set up on the market site.

Cattle market – sheep sales today!

The Grand Union Canal, the same canal that had a branch flowing through Aylesbury, was no longer a main artery for traffic.

When my parents were young there was very little traffic on the roads and a stretch of the Watling Street, just outside Fenny Stratford, was known to the youth of the town as the "Monkey Run."

Boys would walk along one side of the road, girls the other, eyeing one another, joking and flirting. It was where my parents first started to get to know one another. The rest is history.

The local River Ouzel was not only a popular river for anglers. It was also where many, including my father, learned to swim. These boys here are having fun.

Industry included brick making, and the railway was a major

employer in the town. In Fenny Stratford, Akroyd Stuart manufactured one of the first heavy oil engines.

Brush manufacturing began in the late 19th century and continued for over 60 years. Fenny Stratford's other industries included a timber yard and saw mill, a printing works, tea packing factory, and an iron foundry.

Fenny Stratford also contained one of Britain's first telephone repeater stations. The station was powered by a locally produced Akroyd Stuart engine. Repeater stations were necessary, as early long-distance telephone circuits had to be amplified around every 50 miles.

During World War II, as everyone now knows, Bletchley Park was the centre of secret decoding operations. At the time, all the local residents knew was that some kind of top-secret war work was being carried out there, as that was obvious. It did mean a temporary influx of residents in the area for the duration of the war.

Bletchley Park Manor House

Operating "Colossus"

Bletchley Park housed the Post Office Management School after WWII and is now home to the National Museum of Computing.

By mid-1952 the Council had agreed terms with five London Boroughs to accept people and businesses from bombed-out sites in London. This trend, known as the London Overspill, continued through the 1950s and 1960s, both the permanent population and the economy correspondingly growing.

Bletchley continued to expand and its economy prosper until the early 1970s. In 1971 the combined population of Bletchley and Fenny Stratford was 30, 642. But in the late 1960s it had become a suburb of the new city of Milton Keynes.

Parts of the town were cut off from one another by new road building. Cambridge Street and Western Road had been one continuous thoroughfare but a dual carriageway was built that sliced them in two.

There was also no longer a direct access to Buckingham Road through the town. These are among the reasons why Dad had no desire to visit Bletchley in later life.

With the opening of Central:MK, Milton Keynes' shopping mall, Bletchley went into a commercial decline. But there are plans for revival, with a large sports and event stadium there already.

STEWARTBY VILLAGE

The Stewart family had been directors of the London Brick Company from 1900. They were instrumental in developing the brickworks at Stewartby, which had grown into the biggest in the world by the time we were there. There were more than thirty brick kiln chimneys when we moved to Stewartby. They made a real landmark, especially as four of the central chimneys had, respectively: L, B, C (for London Brick Company) and STEWARTBY written on them in large white letters.

Even though the chimneys were so tall, when there was no wind and atmospheric conditions were right the smoke sank to the ground, shrouding the bottom of the village. It didn't affect us so badly where we lived but even so the smell of sulphur could be awful at times.

The brick company owned a lot of land around the area. It meant that when one knothole (clay pit) was exhausted they could start digging out another. The laboratory in Stewartby tested the quality of everything, from the clay right through to the finished article; bricks, roofing tiles, hollow blocks and field drainpipes.

Exterior facing bricks, unlike plain interior ones, were made in different colours and textures. Very hard "Rustic" bricks, a pleasant red in colour and rough textured, were used to build all the village houses.

The Stewarts built a so-called model village on the site of the tiny hamlet of Wootton Pillinge, providing homes for the brickyard workers. The first phase of 210 houses, started in 1926, was completed by the beginning of WWII. It was excellent company housing for workers in those days.

The construction was of high quality, of course using the brickworks' own products. Mains water and electricity were brought into the village, although oddly enough not gas. Every house had an indoor toilet and bathroom (not universal then) and a garden.

The village footpaths were made from pieces of broken clay tile, in its various shades of mellow deep red, set in cement. The look was very unusual and pleasing to the eye. When simply walking you hardly noticed the slight unevenness of the surface, although it was different when pushing a pram - or riding a bike or roller skates.

Stewartby initially comprised one long street running up the village, deviating at intervals to wind around in four "Closes." In these closes the houses were arranged around the road, which bordered a central grassy area. There was no other road exit from them, except for Montgomery Close. From the back of that you could take a road left down to the "New Houses," a small estate built behind the main road some years later.

The largest house in the village, where the works manager lived, was near the club. This was quite separate from the other village houses. The brickworks, club, village hall and Co-op shop (incorporating the post office) were all at the bottom end of the village. Then houses ran along both sides of Stewartby Way, on the flat ground from the brickworks end, as far as a lane just before the school. After that the road started to run uphill.

From this point the ordinary houses were only built on the left side of the road, opposite the school, up to the main London - Bedford railway line. This was known to us all as the Bedpan Line because from Bedford it ran into St Pancras station in London.

Running uphill from the school opposite these houses, in the curve of The Crescent, was a big grassy area. When I was a child only four large houses stood on The Crescent, two detached and two semi-detached, just beyond the school.

Their residents have included at various times the LBC's Chief Chemist, Chief Engineer, Head Planner, the Stewartby Secondary School Head Teacher, and the Scottish Free Church minister.

The ground levelled out again at the roundabout by the top end of The Crescent. There was a wide grassy area between the footpath and main road through the village, on both sides at the bottom end.

Here some large old trees grew, together with younger lime trees planted by the company. Then on the left, where the footpath and grassy area continued, just a row of lime trees marched all the way up the village.

It was after World War II that the main road through the village was named Stewartby Way and the closes called Churchill, Alexander, Montgomery and Wavell, as tributes to those wartime leaders.

The senior school became what was known as a Secondary Modern School. Its entrance was on The Crescent, whereas the building housing the infant and junior schools, although next to it, was actually set back just behind a small grassed area facing Stewartby Way.

The building of the first of the Sir Malcolm Stewart Homes, in one of which my parents later lived, was completed in 1956.

We lived on the corner of Wavell Close and Stewartby Way.

Wavell Close from Stewartby Way
199 is out of view, right front.

Across Stewartby Way was Carter's Farm. Between the farm and the railway embankment were a number of allotments, one of which Dad worked while still able, and then a footpath along which blackberry brambles and dog roses grew.

The roundabout in 1959, Carter's Farm behind it on the right. Beyond is the railway embankment.

Looking down the village from the roundabout in the same year.

All the roundabout planting was done by the groundsmen for as long as the London Brick Company owned the village.

The houses on the corners of Alexander and Wavell Close were next largest in size to those on The Crescent and were semi-detached, whereas most in the village were terraced.

We lived in one of these corner houses on Wavell Close. One on Alexander Close was the village police house. Stewartby had its own village constable (bobby). What was our brick shed, opposite the back door, was his office.

Across a side road from the sports ground was Stewartby United Church. One of the doctors from the GP practice in nearby Kempston came to hold a surgery in a hut next to the church twice a week. There was also a regular mother and baby clinic held there.

The other small estate of houses, the so-called "New Houses," had been built behind here, running up the hill as far as Montgomery Close.

Groundsmen mowed the grass, planted out the roundabout and took care of the rose beds in the village.

They also cut the thick mass of privet bush outside our house and the other corner houses on Wavell and Alexander Closes, as well as pruning trees and any other gardening work.

The whole village looked really lovely. All the houses were kept in excellent condition too, with any problems taken care of by maintenance men employed by the brick company. It really was in many ways a truly "model" village.

Stewartby was served by two bus routes, one at each end of the village, and by the Bletchley to Bedford rail service.

Stewartby Halt with its crossing keeper's hut, bank of manual signal levers and the low platform. The crossing keeper's house is just behind the hut.

The village was designed to be self-contained. There were the Co-op grocery shop come post office, the company owned and heavily subsidised workingmen's club, sports ground with bowling green and other games facilities, the village hall, church, and the infant, junior and senior schools.

The village hall had a beehive carved in relief above the big entrance doors. I think this was to symbolise Stewartby as a hive of industry.

The London Brick Company, although it was a limited (public) company, was basically run by the Stewart family who owned a controlling interest.

The Stewart family was very paternalistic, the Stewarts genuinely concerned for the wellbeing of their employees and families. They even considered the schooling needs of the children in surrounding villages. And Sir Malcolm Stewart set up a trust fund in his will to provide free sheltered housing for company pensioners and widows.

That is not to say that the founding London Brick Company Stewart, Sir Halley, was not controlling. For example, being very Calvinistic he would not allow washing to be hung out on a line on a Sunday.

To break this rule meant eviction! But overall, employees and their families got a good deal from the company. And the strict rules died along with Sir Halley, some years before our move to Stewartby.

When Hanson took over the London Brick Company in 1984, rent for my parents had gone up to just £9 per week, still subsidised. But the days of subsidised rent then became a thing of the past as the houses were sold off, with first refusal going to existing tenants.

Sadly, in February 2008 brickmaking at Stewartby came to an end. Hanson closed the brickworks. The chimneys did not meet UK sulphur emission regulations, despite meeting those of the European Union.

The brickworks chimneys have almost all been demolished and the works site lies derelict. But the village itself has expanded and remains a thriving community of old timers and new comers alike. There are plans too for yet more houses to be built on the old brickworks site.

PRE-DECIMAL CURRENCY

In England after 1066 the Normans used their own French coins, each impressed with a small star. Norman French for little star was *esterlin*.

The pound sterling was a pound weight of *esterlin*, roughly 240 coins. So *esterlin* became Anglicised to sterling, which became the name for the whole currency. The coin itself was called a penny, its pre-Conquest name.

Pennies are believed to be named after King Penda of Mercia. Shilling comes from the old English "to divide," from when coins were often cut to make smaller denominations.

Pre-decimal currency was, as I've said previously, sometimes called LSD, written £ s d. The pound symbol is an ornate L, from the Latin libra - a pound. The s comes from a Roman coin, the solidus. The penny symbol was d for denarius, also a Roman coin.

This is how prices were written and spoken. Two shillings and sixpence (a half crown) would be 2/6, and could be said as "two and six" or "half a crown." You would not normally say the words "shillings" and "pence."

If the amount was a pound or larger, you'd say just the "pounds." So one pound seven shillings and sixpence would be written £3/7/6, and would be spoken as "Three pounds, seven and six." Or you might see £3/7/- and say "Three pounds seven."

If the amount was less than a pound and there were no pence, then you wrote a dash and did say "shillings." For example: 4/-, spoken as "four shillings." The Mad Hatter in Alice in Wonderland has a price tag on his hat saying "In This Style 10/6." So this hat would cost ten shillings and sixpence (said as "ten and six").

There were notes for 10/- and for £1, £5 on upwards, all different sizes and colours, all much larger than today's bank notes. Silver coins were half crowns, florins (worth 2 shillings), shillings and sixpenny pieces (sixpences).

Copper coins were thrupenny (thr'penny) bits worth, as their name suggests, three pence (thr'pence); pennies; half pennies, commonly called ha'pennies (pronounced with a long a) and farthings, quarters of a penny. A crown (worth 5/-), was no longer in common usage when I was a child and nor was the sovereign coin, worth £1. But the farthing was.

Some prices were still written in guineas, although the guinea coin itself was also obsolete. A guinea was worth £1/1/-. There were slang terms, some still in use such as "quid" for pound, and some now redundant, such as "bob" for shilling, "tanner" for sixpence or "half a dollar" for half a crown. Two pence was always pronounced "tuppence."

Confused? It's easy really!

This system, more sophisticated than the decimal, allowed for much finer gradations of the amounts of money.

Money tables

12d = 1/-	84d = 7/-
18d = 1/6	96d = 8/-
24d = 2/-	108d = 9/-
30d = 2/6	120d = 10/-
36d = 3/-	240d = £1
42d = 3/6	20s = £1
48d = 4/-	100d = 8/4
60d = 5/-	Third of £1 = 6/8
72d = 6/-	Two thirds of £1 = 13/4

Pre-decimal Coins Sterling

All reverse side. Monarch's head on obverse

Farthing   Ha'penny   Penny

Thr'pence   Sixpence   Shilling

Florin (two shillings)   Half a crown

Golden Guinea

IMPERIAL WEIGHTS AND MEASURES

Weights went from ounces, through pounds, stones and hundredweight, to tons. You will know some of these, especially those still in official use in the US and common use in the UK. This weight system is specifically known as "avoirdupois," pronounced as the French, from Middle English words meaning goods sold by weight.

The measurement system for weight, length and area is known as Imperial and temperature was measured on the Fahrenheit scale. The main length and area measurements, such as inches, feet, yards and miles, are still used for many purposes. Others are archaic but some of them, such as a "chain" length for a wicket on a cricket pitch, are still in specialised use.

Here are tables of the measures Dad used and that we also had to learn:

<u>Length</u>
12 inches = 1 foot
3 feet = 1 yard   5280 feet = 1 mile
5.5 yards = 1 rod, pole or perch
22 yards (4 pole) = 1 chain   1760 yards = 1 mile
10 chains = 1 furlong   8 furlongs = 1 mile

<u>Area</u>
144^2 inches = 1^2 foot
9^2 feet = 1^2 yard
4840^2 yards = 1 acre
640 acres = 1^2 mile

A pole or rod was originally the length of the rod a mediaeval ploughman used to poke or tap the ox or horse pulling his plough.

Perch is a corruption of the Roman measurement perdica, the length of a long Roman spear and later the length of a pike. In this instance, neither perch nor pike refers to the fish of that name!

Rods, poles and perches are also, somewhat confusingly, a measure of area. In this usage, one rod, pole or perch equals 30.25^2 yards, the length measurement squared. This was never specified: presumably it was taken for granted that you would know by the context whether length or area.

Mass
16 ounces (oz) = 1 pound (lb)
14 pounds = 1 stone
8 stones (112 lb) = 1 hundredweight [cwt]
20 cwt = 1 ton (2240 lb)

Capacity
5 fluid ounces = 1 gill
20 fluid ounces = 1 pint
4 gills = 1 pint
2 pints = 1 quart
4 quarts = 1 gallon

Volume
1728^3 inches = 1^3 foot
27^3 feet = 1^3 yard

It was partly to cope with all these different measures, including the currency, that many generations learned their 2 through 12, 14 and 16 times tables by rote in junior school.

You know what I mean: 1 times 2 is 2, 2 times 2 is 4 etc, chanted in singsong voices. Everyone learned by heart, too, how many feet and yards in a mile, a quarter of a mile and half a mile, as well as many of the other measurements.

The difference between the UK and US systems seems strange. For so long, the monetary system in the UK was alien to the US. Now the UK has a decimal system for currency and has also changed some other measures too. And now people in the US will be finding these other measures alien instead, including temperature measurements.

I still often think in Fahrenheit, which of course everyone also learned, even though I do use Centigrade, the official system in the UK now and here in New Zealand. That is another measure where the old one was more sophisticated, allowing for finer gradation, with 180 degrees Fahrenheit between freezing and boiling, rather than the "mere" 100 degrees in Centigrade or its slightly more exact version, Celsius.

AFTERWORD

Jack's story is told and I hope that I have done some small justice to his life and memory, to his love of family and to his own family history.

There were some things concerning my father's wartime experiences that obviously deeply affected him, and of which he would or could not speak.

Right up to his death there were programmes he wouldn't watch or listen to. Some of these programmes were too emotional and painful for him. Some glorified war, a sentiment he could not abide.

He lived his life by his principles, but always with kindness, love and consideration for others.

If my life turns out to have been half as well lived as that of my father, I shall rest content.

This book, with its reminders of the events and trauma my father and many others endured throughout WWII, was being written during another very difficult time for the world. 2020 has been the year of Covid-19, a pandemic almost beyond the imagining of recent generations.

I now live in New Zealand, far from the land of both my birth and that of my father. Last year John and I gained our citizenship, after living in Christchurch since 2014. Here is where we shall see out our days.

I am very grateful that this country is almost insulated from the effects of the pandemic, that our Prime Minister and government took firm and effective action soon after the outset. Since a very early lockdown life in Christchurch has felt quite normal, though we are required to take a few precautions.

However, with family and friends in other countries I have not been altogether insulated personally from the impact of Covid-19.

Even as I continued to write at the beginning of this year, 2021, the number of cases and deaths where they live was still rising alarmingly. Sadly, those numbers are still rising at a frightening rate in some countries. But thankfully my loved ones and friends have remained safe and well.

There is also finally some hope of an end to the dreadfulness, with vaccination programmes being rolled out in a number of countries. But I fear it will still be a very long time before any kind of real normality returns to our planet.

RESOURCES

Bedford Borough Council's Marston Vale Oral History Project 2001-2005, "Changing Landscapes: Changing Lives." The tape recordings and their transcriptions, with written summaries of each interview, plus associated photographs, are available to the public by prior arrangement with the Forest Centre at Marston Moretaine, Bedfordshire.

"Jack Blane's Wartime Memoir" is my spoken account on YouTube of his own war story, with a slide show of wartime pictures.

Information about Aylesbury Gaol, and the photographs, are found in an article in the "Tatler" issue 121, 21 October 1903.

Entering www.mkweb.co.uk into your browser takes you to a website where there is information on the history of the area around Bletchley and Fenny Stratford, as well as the present-day new city of Milton Keynes.

Typing "Marston Vale Brickies" into your search engine should bring up a site including all kinds of information on Stewartby and the brickworks, even a panorama of the village to scroll around.

A book entitled "Bletchley Voices," by Robert Cook, Tempus Publishing Ltd 1998, is an oral history with people telling their own memories of the town. Dad, His brothers Donald and Martin, and Martin's wife Gwen, were all contributors.

If you are interested in railway history and anecdotes you might like "A Railway Man's Tales of Old Bletchley" by A E Grigg. This was published by Baron Birch in a limited edition so it isn't easy to find.

Censuses are an excellent resource. Family Search and Free BMD are both good sites for making a start, and Wikipedia is always a useful source of information.

But for family history there's no beating a real historian, such as Rob Schafer!

Finally, there are my own autobiographical books.

"Bucks, Beds and Bricks," my childhood memoir, was published to Amazon in 2011.

"In No Particular Order," containing stories of my later life along with other writings, was published in 2019, also to Amazon.

I can be contacted at jeanauthor03@gmail.com

Printed in Great Britain
by Amazon